Say

YES

to

NO

DOUBLEDAY

New York   London   Toronto
Sydney   Auckland

Say

YES

to

NO

Using the Power of
NO
to Create the Best
in Life, Work, and Love

GREG COOTSONA

CD

DOUBLEDAY

Published in the United States by Doubleday, an imprint of The Doubleday Publishing Group, a division of Random House, Inc., New York

DOUBLEDAY and the DD colophon are trademarks of Random House, Inc.

Book design by Michael Collica

ISBN 978-1-60751-827-3

PRINTED IN THE UNITED STATES OF AMERICA

To Laura, Melanie, and Elizabeth
Three Great Yeses in My Life

CONTENTS

Contents

Say

YES

to

NO

Discovering the Power of No (and the Peril of Saying Yes to Everything)

We all want progress, but if you're on the wrong road,
progress means doing an about-turn and walking back to
the right road; in that case, the man who turns back soonest
is the most progressive.

—C. S. LEWIS

———————————•———————————

I'm all right now. My health is excellent. I'm enjoying work and finding more time to play. I'm not dogged by anger. Laura and I are happy, and we're savoring every hour with our two girls.

All this because I started saying yes to no. I've learned to say no to certain demands at work, and I've learned that no creates healthy friendships, marriages, and families. I've discovered that no guards vital commitments and, when used properly, creates excellence. I realize this may sound a bit too wonderful, but compared with where I was a few years ago, life is pretty good.

Fear. New York. March 22, 2001. Thirty-eight years old. Electrodes taped to my chest, running on a treadmill. A cardiologist and her assistant at my side, monitoring my EKG. All this a result of an annual visit to my M.D.: "You're developing elevated blood pressure. We'll probably have to prescribe beta-blockers. But there may be more. The pains in your chest may be due to something more harmful."

Me on blood pressure medicine? *Get serious.* Exercise, good nutrition, prayer, and a positive outlook can solve any problem, right? That's what the self-help books told me. Still, I couldn't deny the chest pains. I also couldn't dispute an alarming experience a few months earlier. I was suddenly awakened at 4:00 a.m. by a racing heart and shortness of breath, my head spinning with unfinished tasks at home and at work. Feeling faint and unable to stand or even lie down, I hunched on my bedroom floor, my head tucked below my heart, waiting a full forty minutes for my pulse to normalize.

"The short- and long-term effects of high blood pressure can be serious," my doctor said. As a pastor, and just someone who reads the newspaper, I'd heard one too many stories about a thirty-something father dropping dead at the dinner table in front of his horrified wife and children. And then there was the ad I'd recently read: "You're 55% more likely to have a heart attack if you live in New York City." *Thanks for that valuable statistic.*

I remember pondering the following question: Is it simply the environment that creates the people? In his movie *Manhattan,* Woody Allen describes New Yorkers as creatures "constantly creating those unnecessary neurotic problems for themselves because it keeps them from dealing with more unsolvable, terrifying problems about the universe."

Maybe. Maybe not. All I knew was my body was kvetching.

So I unwillingly submitted myself to my doctor's referral: "To be sure your heart's all right, I want you to get a full exam from a cardiologist."

I left my doctor's office and began to think back seven years to how this mess started.

In the final stage of my doctorate, I started applying for gainful employment. In May 1994 the perfect interim position opened in my home church in Berkeley. I eagerly applied and got the job. That academic year, I directed the college group of bright students from Cal while I shared a job (and literally a desk, a phone, and a secretary) with a great colleague. Then the permanent position opened in the spring of 1995. Wasn't that thoughtful of God to make my job search so easy? Church members and staff urged me to apply. The message was clear. It was a perfect fit, and everyone knew it. So I eagerly interviewed, figuring I'd soon have the post and wrap up my degree by that December.

But the fun was about to end. It should have struck me as a sign that toward the end of the search process—in fact, around 10:00 one evening—I looked out the front window of my home to see a hiring-committee member (and friend) illuminated by a streetlight, riding his bike up my front walk. *Emile, this is Oakland, California—what are you doing out so late on your bike?* We talked in the front room of my apartment. "I'm sorry, Greg. You were a great candidate—and you know I really like you—but you're not going to get the job."

I sat with the disappointment for a while, a little incredulous and even more angry. Eventually, the church presented a consolation prize: a position as music director for the Sunday evening worship service, where loads of college students attended. At ten hours a week and a salary hovering just above minimum wage, it wasn't what you would call my dream job. To make matters worse, one of my first duties was to lead the music team during the installation ceremony of the goofball who got the job I really wanted.

More disappointment followed. That November a committee read the final draft of my dissertation and commented: "If you had a job to go to, we'd pass you. Since you don't, and since the project really needs to be tightened up, why not revise it and we'll graduate you in May?" My reply was *Yes, of course.* During the next six months, I engaged in a fruitless job search and carefully polished my "masterpiece" while consoling myself with thoughts of van Gogh's relative lack of popularity during his life.

I did finish the dissertation, and the committee green-lighted me for the degree. By the end of May 1996, I had gained a new title, "Dr." Perhaps my life was improving. Just a few weeks later, three different churches called me for interviews. One was the prestigious Fifth Avenue Presbyterian Church, which soon offered me a position as associate pastor for new programs. Suddenly I had the opportunity to live in a world-class city, read the *New York Times* right in Gotham itself, oversee an excellent education program, be a truly cosmopolitan pastor, and, best of all, get paid! Besides that, it was a challenge. *And I love challenges.* To paraphrase Frank Sinatra's famous song for the ecclesiastically minded: "If you can save 'em there, you can save 'em anywhere." I jumped at the offer.

Would it be ungrateful to say that this job offer didn't resolve all my difficulties? Growing up in an unchurched family and spending four years after college owning my own business, I felt apprehensive about my ordination. I simply wasn't ready to be marked as a churchman. Emerging from the safe cocoon of graduate study I had inhabited for the past eight years, I felt excited but ambivalent about the new position. The ambivalence transmuted to anxiety as we planned to move cross-country the very week after my ordination service. Adding to these mixed feelings, as the leaders of my local presbytery laid their hands on me at the culmination of the service, my father-in-law, Fred, lay comatose in a hospital bed as a result of his second stroke in less than ten months. He died the next day. My first official duty as a minister was his funeral. I choked out the homily through tears and a throat worn raw by inadequate sleep. That night I wanted nothing more than to curl up into a fetal position and go to sleep.

We arrived in New York in December, and that first winter—though mild by Gotham's standards—froze our California bones. We were slowed by the bittersweet feelings of leaving our home state, our friends, and our family, and Laura was hobbled by her father's death. The pace of settling in was glacial, the mood bleak. That month we celebrated the birthday of our daughter, Melanie, with a hodgepodge event attended by just one friend of ours who happened to be visiting. The high point consisted in blowing out two meager candles on a cake with a cardboard box as a table.

That first Christmas came, and a treasure trove of family traditions filled our heads . . . without family around. For that first New York Noel, Laura's mother sent us a wreath. It was tradition that every year a circle of fresh Vermont evergreens hung above our mantel just as it did in Laura's parents' house. Now that her father was gone, this symbol loomed large. Oddly, UPS seemed unaware of our wishes and customs. The driver arrived at the door, didn't see a nameplate with "Cootsona" on it, and left without even leaving one of those cute yellow Post-its requesting our signature. The wreath was trapped in the matrix of United Parcel Service on Forty-third and Eleventh.

But wait a minute: In Oakland, the wreath had always arrived on our doorstep with plenty of time for the holidays. Here, twenty-five hundred miles closer to Vermont, the UPS driver couldn't find our apartment, because we didn't have a nameplate or a doorman to sign for us. *Welcome to New York City.*

Unable to convince the Boys in Brown to make another delivery, Laura urgently telephoned me one afternoon at work, insisting that I negotiate the complicated Manhattan bus system and find this package—no mean feat for a newcomer to the big city. On a chilly December afternoon, I located the UPS distribution center hidden among the warehouses of Hell's Kitchen. Eventually convincing the right person that I was indeed Greg Cootsona, I retrieved the wreath. With my prize in hand, I found transportation uptown and appeared at home, eagerly presenting the package to Laura. Soon the wreath hung over the living room mantel. It was pretty. It was green and Christmassy. We stared at it, hoping to magically elicit some healing balm from the evergreen fronds. It didn't work. This memory of home didn't compensate for the friends we had left behind. And it certainly didn't bring Laura's dad back to life.

As the calendar turned to 1997, we set ourselves to the task of setting up our brownstone apartment on the Upper West Side. For non–New Yorkers, this takes a bit of explaining. You might imagine walking to the garage to find the station wagon waiting. You drive to IKEA, pick up the perfect lamp, cart it home, and set it up. But in Manhattan, the car isn't parked outside. It's two blocks away in a garage (largely collecting dust and grime at the rate of $350 a month). Driving requires finding a parking space on the street (with about the same odds as winning the Lotto) or in a garage at $22.50 an hour. If driving wasn't an option, there were always cabs (when you could find one), and that meant $20 round-trip . . . which seemed a bit overpriced when the errand consisted of $1.50 of nuts and bolts. And then the bus and subway . . . Ultimately, we schlepped a lot on foot, braving New York wind and rain and resorting to some odd means of transport.

One windy day, I remember a ten-block walk home from Ace Hardware, balancing a sheet of four-by-six-foot Plexiglas—which we needed to cover dangerous, non-child-friendly gaps in our staircase railing—on the jogger stroller while pushing my two-and-a-half-year-old, Melanie. The wind that whipped between the concrete towers of the Upper West Side blew this beautiful, clear sail and turned us into land-bound windsurfers. The only inherent problem here was sharing the road with MTA buses and yellow cabs, which was, in a word, terrifying. (I write this now with a certain incredulity: Laura and I were yet two years away from the greatest Manhattan discovery of all—home delivery.)

Every day Laura seemed to walk in cement. She was grieving and despondent. We both felt lonely. I tried adjusting to my first job as an ordained minister in a church. People insisted on calling me "The Reverend Doctor Gregory S. Cootsona." In California, I was simply "Greg" . . . or "dude." The mantle of my new calling hung heavily on my shoulders. As the months progressed, I struggled to make it through days that often found me home at 11:00 p.m. The hours seemed too long, but I was surrounded by this hyperkinetic city and parishioners who customarily log in twelve-hour days and naturally assume that their pastors do the same. "Why are you still at work?" was not a phrase that came quickly to their lips.

Yes, New York City certainly challenged me. It wasn't the most welcoming environment for spiritual development. The most important concession the city makes to faith is to suspend parking regulations on religious holidays. (Usually one side of the street has no parking on Tuesdays and Thursdays, the other

Mondays and Wednesdays, but on Rosh Hashanah and Christmas Day you can park on whichever side you please.) This reality led the *New York Times* to declare on its Web page: "You're a New Yorker when . . . everything you know about religion you learned from parking rules."

Laura continued as a fund-raising consultant almost immediately after the move. I now see that fact as amazing, not only in light of the grief over her father's death, but also because of the difficulty of her pregnancy just four months after we arrived. She, too, tried to hold together the demands of parenthood and career while maintaining sanity—all the more difficult in an age that promotes the über-Frau as the apex of true womanhood.

All this means that Laura was physically present, but, to use a sanitized psychological expression, she was "emotionally unavailable"—fogged by her sadness and soon slowed by her pregnancy. Consequently, I felt I couldn't share the frustrations of my new job. (It was supposed to be wonderful anyway.) I felt abandoned, walking alone on a thin board as floodwaters rose on both sides. Soon the sadness spread—or rather hollowed me out—first in my chest and then from my eyes to my guts, an empty, metallic feeling. I felt like the Tin Man dancing on that narrow, treacherous plank . . . without the cute dance moves and sonorous voice.

In movies, grief is attended by swelling violins and decisive insights. But that's only in movies. For Laura and me, it was a numbing experience that began pushing us apart. We silently became overwhelmed. The grieving, the loss, the transition, and our drive to pursue our callings in this world-class city all together sucked us dry. We needed a break and time to move more slowly into this new phase. But no one was handing us rest, and family support was thousands of miles away.

The pressure at work only increased. I was charged with creating a fellowship group to keep the twenty-somethings—who composed 65 percent of our new members (and soon numbered over a thousand)—interested in the church. Our retreat in April 1997 totaled seven, including an intern and me. Hardly an impressive showing. In addition, I soon became initiated into the famous combative nature of New Yorkers. My first major disagreement with a board member (an elder) happened as I returned to work, exhausted after slogging through mud one Easter week to build houses in rural Maine. It didn't matter that we disagreed—or that we later became fast friends—the point was that I was fighting so early. The phone call left me angry and despairing, wondering why I had moved away from family and friends to this godforsaken city. *Oh yeah, that's right. There was no job back in the Bay Area.*

In January 1998, our second child, Lizzie, was born. Some say that two is more than twice as hard as one. I don't know. I just know the sum of this new baby's demands was often too much. The mounting pressures of work, marriage, and family seemed to narrow my veins and constrict my blood flow.

Indeed my life carried too many responsibilities, and at times I became inexplicably frustrated. I contacted a psychoanalyst (now feeling like a true New Yorker!), clearly establishing that I had only enough time and money for six appointments. Could we go forward? "Sure." Though I was comforted to talk about my problems every two weeks, frankly it didn't offer much insight. At the end of the sixth session, the analyst assured me, "I think we're really doing great work. Now we are getting somewhere. It would be good from here out to meet twice a week." I declined this gracious offer with the question lurking in my mind: *Which part of "six appointments" didn't you understand?*

This is not to say that everything was bad.

Yet, in time, almost everything in my work life turned

around. And perhaps my success contributed even further to my wake-up call. I had said yes to too many requests. (As is typical for many people, my reward for success was to receive more demands.) Our education program, the Center for Christian Studies, continued to expand to a pace of eighty to ninety classes a year with over two thousand registrants. I took on the task of teaching seven or eight classes a year with titles like "Bringing Belief to Life: The Apostles' Creed" and "Philosophy for Understanding Theology: Plato and Aristotle." Exciting—I soon had interviews about the classes with *New York* magazine, which later labeled our program "one of the best bargains in adult education in New York City." I received a forty-five-thousand-dollar grant from the Louisville Institute to help promote our new "academy" model of education throughout the country. The *Wall Street Journal* and a Swiss news company (whose name I forgot—it became a blur) interviewed me on a Faith@Work series titled "Faith, Hope, and Love in the New Economy," put together after the collapse of the dot-coms. The BBC, the *New York Times,* and MetroGuide New York (a cable station) all were fascinated by the hordes of twenty-somethings streaming in the doors.

Nevertheless, I was depleted. It was no surprise that my body showed signs of deep fatigue. The diagnosis of mild hypertension frightened but did not surprise me. I was clearly in need of a change.

On that crisp March morning in 2001, I walked on East Seventy-fourth Street to the cardiologist's office for my stress test, and I suppose I even bargained a little with God: *I've made changes. If you let me off the hook, I'll continue to take time for my health. I'll learn how not to push beyond what I'm capable of. Help me.*

I entered the waiting room and filled out forms, guaranteeing my unwillingness to sue (should I drop dead during the stress test) and my ability to pay (my medical insurance was good). After entering the exam room, I stripped down from my gray business suit to a T-shirt, pulled on warm-up pants, and laced up my cross-trainers. The technician strapped electrodes to my chest, and I started walking. As I glanced at the walls of this small room, I saw numerous posters from athletes, one from a three-time-world-champion water-skier: "Thanks, Molly, for all you've done." After a few minutes, Dr. Stephenson walked in. We exchanged basic info. She said, "Start jogging," and I did. The duo gradually increased the speed of the machine and thus my heart rate. They consulted the monitors and wrote on clipboards. I started actually running and grew progressively more winded and curious. *How high would they let my heartbeat go? Would I fail the test? Could this count as my workout for the day?*

The transforming moment came when I hit my maximum rate. Dr. Stephenson let me stay there long enough to prove it wasn't a fluke and then progressively slowed the machine. I jumped off sweaty, feeling I had mounted a new pinnacle of health. Still, I required the expert's opinion: "Molly" (I was beginning to feel triumphant and friendly), "what did you find?" She gave the verdict: "You're in excellent physical shape. Your heart is great. No problem there. Any health issue lies somewhere else. Probably an issue with your blood pressure. Exercise, eat well, and watch your stress level. Then check in with your GP. See how that works."

Exhilarated, I barely had time to throw on my suit, pay the bill, and check out. I ran triumphantly onto that crowded, busy Manhattan sidewalk. I was Archimedes shouting "Eureka." I had found the enemy that lurked inside and that threatened my health, my family, and my dreams. I had answered yes to far too many voices. I couldn't keep up the pace, and I had not recognized the signs of danger. That day it became abundantly clear that I had been given a second chance. I was going to change my life. The first task at hand: reevaluate every responsibility I had said yes to.

Are you overtaxed? Do you find yourself complaining: "There's just no time for what I want to do?" Is it difficult for you to say no? Does your work lack healthy rhythm? Does it incessantly drive your life? Are your friendships and family relationships impoverished? Do you want to find a spiritual center?

This book describes what I discovered when I started saying yes to no. But in order to gain wider perspectives, I've consulted scores of people about the principles in this book: CEOs, investment bankers, business consultants, stay-at-home parents, artists, and students. Some are type A personalities; others could have written *The 7 Habits of Highly Ineffective People*. Some feel focused in their lives but are overly busy. Some are unable to figure out how to bring their lives together. In order to gain the perspective of history, I've scoured classic books, thereby "interviewing" great philosophers, world leaders, and writers. Their stories are woven through these pages.

In talking with women and men over the past few years about the power of no, I continued to hear a set of questions:

- Will saying no turn me into a negative person?
- Will I miss out on opportunities at work?
- Does no prevent me from finding enduring friendships and romantic relationships?
- Will people still like me? Will I have friends?

- How do I know when to say no?
- After no, then what?

This book answers those questions and offers ways to stay sane in an increasingly frantic world. Each chapter includes practical tips and exercises so that you can experiment with the power of no.

By saying yes to no, I've discovered keys to a successful life, not lived under unrelenting pressure, but with the rhythms of health and wholeness. I want you to experience these discoveries. Saying no isn't about sloth and negativity. It's about establishing boundaries that guard important values. In the following pages, I'll discuss the power of no in three key areas: personal life, work, and love. When that triangle is well-balanced, we find health and peace.

Essentially, I believe we can live a positive life by saying no at pivotal moments. Ultimately, our nos only create space for a deeper yes to be declared, and conversely the great yeses of life define our nos. No is definitely not the ultimate word. Beyond it, we are designed to listen to a still, small voice whispering yes to what truly matters. Ultimately, it's not even the yes that we pronounce. It's the yes we hear and follow fearlessly. With that in mind, I'd like to tell you a story.

One evening, my friend Mark's six-year-old, Sam, was taking a bath. Mark entered the bathroom to remove Sam from the tub and dry him off for bed.

"Just a minute, Dad. God's talking to me."

Being a reflective type, Mark figured this was a good thing. "Okay. I'll wait." He went over to the toilet and sat there for a minute or two, wondering what his son would reveal.

"Okay. I'm ready."

As he wrapped Sam in a towel and dried off his ears and hair, Mark asked, "What did God say?" He expected perhaps some extended revelation (of the type, it seems, that come only to children).

Sam, however, uttered one simple word.

"Yes."

That was it.

Beyond all our nos, and even our yeses, is the ultimate yes from a voice greater than ours. When we hear that yes, we have truly discovered an unfathomable power.

PART ONE

Personal Life

CHAPTER ONE

Michelangelo and the Marble
The Art of Negation

I saw the angel in the marble and carved until I set him free.

—MICHELANGELO BUONARROTI, sculptor,
painter, architect, and (in the eyes of many)
creator of the Renaissance

———————————— • ————————————

The story goes something like this: An admirer ran up to Michelangelo and asked how he sculpted the famous statue of David that now sits in Accademia Gallery in the city of Florence. How did he craft this masterpiece of form and beauty? What was he thinking? How did he work with the rock so that he produced this exquisite human figure?

Michelangelo replied with this strikingly simple description: First, he said, I fixed my attention on the slab of raw marble. I studied it, sketched a few simple pencil drawings on it, and then "chipped away all that wasn't David."

The questioner was stunned. When pressed to go further, the

artist offered an explanation: "In every block of marble I see a statue as though it stood before me, shaped and perfected in attitude and action. I have only to hew away the rough walls that imprison the lovely apparition to reveal it to the other eyes as mine see it." He discerned, imprisoned inside the crude block, a beauty that had to be released. And so he labored with all the genius and persistence he could muster. And what emerged from the rock has amazed and fascinated viewers ever since. Some even call it the greatest sculpture that ever existed.

Michelangelo unveiled beauty through what he removed. His was the art of negation. He created through the power of no.

I find that I'm often careless and haphazard at chipping away the excess in my life. I don't tap away in order to craft what's essential and crucial in myself. Instead, I add. And unlike with marble, humans have the choice to attach more and more blocks of unformed matter to our daily lives. Many times we become bored and abandon our project when just the hint of the beauty is peering out of the rock. Or we never get started. We stare at the raw, unformed marble and freeze before the tasks that stare back at us.

And then, to complicate matters, we live surrounded by a culture of almost countless possibilities. And so, paralyzed by choice, we can't decide what to cut out. To commit—to work on one's stone—means to say no to the overwhelming majority of these alluring possibilities. The options mock the hint of limits, and setting boundaries comes across as a mere suggestion. Consequently, many of us remain unformed. Many never find the life of beauty, excellence, and success that lies within.

Yet some do. Some of us do chip away with precise vision and durable resolve. What makes the difference? What's the secret? How do we move beyond good intentions to form habits that produce integrity and care for others, that craft goals and character in our lives, that make space for the relationships we crave, and that hone skills at work?

The Michelangelo story leads to some reflections on the power of no and how to sculpt our lives for true success. As the master artist phrased it, "The more the marble wastes, the more the statue grows."

How are we blocks of unchiseled marble? Have we succeeded in finding excellence and pursuing it with dogged perseverance? Is there a "you" and "me" hidden in a formless life, waiting to be released? Are we imprisoned in nos yet unstated? Are you letting God, the Creator and Re-creator, transform your life, craft and mold you?

These are some lessons I've learned by studying the great artist, organized into four large blocks: chiseling, creativity, grit, and God.

Chiseling
True success (that is, beauty and excellence) is found in chipping away.

Michelangelo found that he could create his sculpture only by removing what the figure didn't need until it achieved the beauty of its inherent form.

We need to say no to the things in our life that we don't want or need. This is most important when it comes to setting goals.

I've observed three major steps in setting goals. The first step in creating a successful life is to determine your key priorities. What do you really want? Here's the crux: Those goals and plans often lie dormant in the rock unless we start chiseling. Step two: outline your nos. In other words, what will you *not* pursue? It's finding what to say no to. And, finally, step three: sticking by those nos. This is where most people fall down in seeking what's best for their lives. Step three becomes really demanding when other good options present themselves. This is especially true of those things that *seem* like success: goals like wealth, fame, and position. But those things—as I'll describe in the next chapter—are not what really matters. They are secondary goals and can become significant distractions. Instead, true success is to discern the essence of what we're created to be and to follow it relentlessly.

Creativity
Break the mold or see something for the first time and replicate it . . . with variation.

Donatello had created a David sculpture (bronze, in this case) in the 1440s, some sixty years before Michelangelo's. That could have been the final artistic word on this biblical hero. But Michelangelo knew he had something original to offer. And so he took marble, started to sculpt, and took David in a new direction. Donatello crafted his slim, slightly effeminate David after the battle with Goliath, wearing just a hat and holding a sword, with his foot on the giant's head. Michelangelo discarded the silly hat and conferred a new power and vitality to the young warrior, who stands poised before battle, with veins bulging, to take on his gigantic foe.

Looking intently at the *David*'s face, you can see an idealized projection of Michelangelo—not his actual visage, but his driving creativity. Just as he chose to portray David in the sculpture before the battle, looking out to face his enormous foe, this twenty-six-year-old artist seems to be scanning the horizon for his future projects.

Grit
The artist's vision directed his work and provided him
with gritty resolve.

With precision of vision combined with incredible resolve, Michelangelo peered *through* the unformed shape into the figure it could become. This is the artistic concept of *disegno,* meaning "to sketch" or "to draw": The final product must first appear in the artist's imagination. Michelangelo simply knew David—his age, how he was positioned, the shape of his torso, and that beautiful curved left arm just below his chin. Through the amorphous mass of rock, a clear form sparkled in his imagination. The marble would only need chipping away. And so, gradually, tap by tap, *David*—or the *Pietà,* or *Moses,* or the *Dying Slave*—emerged. The glory of Michelangelo's sculpting was that he could see through the raw material, through all the chipping away, to its ultimate destiny. As Michelangelo believed: "The marble not yet carved can hold the form of every thought the greatest artist has."

To be clear: The yes will help guide the vision. And it needs to be decisive. We need to know the voice that guides us. Critical to the process of continuing is to know the direction you're going. To discern that vision, I draw inspiration from a quotation by the noted feminist Naomi Wolf: "Excellence, to me, is the state of grace that can descend only when one tunes out all the world's clamor, listens to an inward voice one recognizes as wiser than one's own, and transcribes without fear." Where do you become quiet enough to hear that wiser voice? In Chapter Three, I have some directions for tuning out the technological static and listening. For now, I want to underline that the yes directs the nos. Our *disegno* directs the chiseling.

My reading of Michelangelo is that he felt that he was simply one of the greatest geniuses alive . . . although this fact also clearly tortured him. Other art, and artists, seem to have spurred him to creativity.

We probably don't proceed with similar conviction—or perhaps with Michelangelo's overinflated ego and distressed soul. Instead, we may feel inadequate for the task of chiseling our lives into something beautiful. Nevertheless, I know I've got to start because it's my life, my work of art. No one else can really do it. And in view of all the lives around you, your vision will be something different, a unique contribution. And though every act of refining our lives through the chiseling power of no may not be a masterpiece, that's okay. The critical decision is to begin.

> *It takes a great deal of time and durable resolve to*
> *finish a job, a journey, a commission.*

Sometimes Michelangelo clearly loved, or hated, the commissions he was given. And they took time. The famous tomb for Julius II at the church of San Pietro in Vincoli presented a recurring forty-year nightmare.

What waits before you? Finishing a degree? A new baby who needs care? Restoring a marriage that's teetering? Or trying to figure out how to write that song that's rolling around in your head? Whatever it is, setting your mind to the task begins the work, and there will be innumerable distractions along the way. What we need is the power to say no and mean it. What we need is determination.

Think of the World Wide Web with its four billion sites. I know what beckons me: Every time I look at this computer screen to type in more of *Say Yes to No* I hear the voice of the Web beckoning, "Surf me. I have so much information and stimulation to offer." Or remember when there were just the three channels of network TV? Now cable tenders hundreds of alternatives. Consider that it used to be coffee, black or with some combo of milk and sugar. Now you can order a 2 percent decaf grande mocha, with or without "whipped."

It's a struggle, and I know it. "No fatigue" enters quickly. To maintain a healthy diet of saying no to distractions challenges me daily. I can be dazzled by all the glittering models for success that our culture parades before me. I intend to live for what really matters for me, but I fail. And so I want to move beyond good intentions to realizing all I can be. I want to succeed at what's really important because, when I'm doing things with excellence, I find happiness. Or there's apathy: I'd rather watch another episode of *24* or surf the Web. Or there's self-doubt: the thought that I simply can't do it. I'll never complete what I started.

Moreover, chipping away takes time. Here I've realized that anything that matters to me is long-term. The *David* took three years. It must have been tedious work. As Michelangelo himself stated, "If people knew how hard I had to work to gain my mastery, it wouldn't seem wonderful at all." Chipping away hurts. The chisel, however, must be harder than the stone. Our resolve must move us forward against the odds.

Yet sometimes we need support. Michelangelo had sixteenth-century popes and the Medici family. He had some deep pockets behind him. But they could also be demanding and capricious.

To be honest, I'm still looking for a patron! (Aren't we all?) But barring some serendipity, a patron, or the fickle face of fame, will never smile on me with undiminished resources. I've found that a surprising number of great artists—and many of us—are still hidden in the folds of history because they never had the backing they needed. (I'll take on that topic soon.) That, however, doesn't diminish their artistic acumen. Nor should we worry if our inner lives are unseen. In order to create a success, you must let go of fame, wealth, and position as preeminent goals. Maybe we have to look for another type of patron, which leads me to the next point.

God

*The quality of your raw material and your source of
creativity are critical.*

Michelangelo's marble had to be chosen carefully for size and composition. Or at least he had to work with the qualities given to him by his raw material. As the artist's fame grew, the marble was supplied to him by some of the richest patrons of the day, but even when he sculpted the *David*, the quality of the stone was mediocre.

We are made of different material, and we can gain confidence by remembering that the Creator is the source of our lives, that God has in fact created each of us with unique talents and gifts. None of us is without flaws, but in the case of the art of our lives, sometimes it's the imperfections that create our most beautiful shapes.

We are God's creations in progress. We are sulpted into who God wants us to become, according to His vision. Michelangelo believed that his creative power reflected divine inspiration. Later he received the moniker Il Divino ("the divine one"), though he was a bit more modest than his fans: "The true work of art is but a shadow of the divine perfection." And I'm convinced my Creator knows what that can look like because God is the supreme artist, who sees our lives as works of art. As the nineteenth-century master painter Vincent van Gogh once wrote, "Christ . . . is more of an artist than the artists; he works in the living spirit and the living flesh; he makes human beings instead of statues." It's definitely more difficult to work with living beings—and to use us in the process of chipping away, since often we resist the chisel. And yet, you might even say that God's chipping away becomes part of the healing of lives.

Saying no through chiseling away at possibilities appears to be God's method. Scientific discoveries have confirmed that this is the way God has created the masterpiece we call our universe. In forming the world, God also chiseled away. The entire universe has come into existence through a gigantic quantity of nos. Since the 1960s, an astounding set of discoveries reveals that the universe has certain, very specific conditions, which allow for the emergence of conscious, moral creatures. Derived from *anthropos,* the Greek word for "human being" (as in "anthropology"), the anthropic principle states that the cosmos is fitted from the beginning for the emergence of life in general and intelligent life in particular. In fact, about thirty discrete, precisely calibrated parameters—such as the expansion rate of the universe, the mass of the universe, the strength of a strong nuclear force, and the ratio of antiprotons to protons—all were needed to produce the universe. Otherwise, it simply would not exist. The Oxford physicist Roger Penrose has described just one such parameter, the "phase-space volume," with a number almost impossible to write—a 1 followed by 10^{123} 0s. That's amazingly precise and signifies an almost innumerable amount of nos.

In other words, the Creator chipped away at an enormous number of possibilities to create this world. God said no many times to create the yeses of life. It looks like the creation of beauty, intelligence, and goodness depends on what is rejected even more than on what is selected. And here's what I figure: If it's good enough for God and the universe, it's good enough for you, me, and our lives.

In sum, as we learn to allow our lives to be shaped—as we learn about chiseling, creativity, grit, and God—a life of beauty emerges. These lessons I take away from Michelangelo and the marble. Michelangelo's image of chipping away and its bearing on creating successful, excellent lives are also paralleled in several other fields. In the next chapter, I will explore how these ideas resonate with seeking to no what's best for us.

CHAPTER TWO

To No What's Best
Creating a Truly Successful Life

*You have reached the pinnacle of success as soon as you
become uninterested in money, compliments, or publicity.*

—THOMAS WOLFE, novelist

———————————•———————————

I t's time to address the topic of success. *Webster's* defines "success" as the "attainment of wealth, favor, or eminence." (I like the word "eminence," don't you? It has a regal air.) Microsoft's Encarta Dictionary includes "impressive achievement, especially in fame, wealth, or position." With those two in mind, and for the sake of this chapter, let's call the trio of *wealth, fame, and position* the world's standard definition of success. It's a definition I'd like to challenge.

Wealth, fame, and position: If you're looking to those three as the keys to the kingdom, as the means to ultimate happiness and fulfillment, I'd recommend another book. Because for me these three do not equal true success. If, however, you're look-

ing for something truly worth living for, then read on. There's
something much more substantial, a path that fulfills our deeper
desires. By using the power of no and negating what *seems* to be
success, we can create a life of beauty and excellence.

So let's redefine success.

True success is being on the right road. I'm adapting a phrase I first
heard from Earl Palmer, the head pastor during my undergradu-
ate days at UC Berkeley (who has just retired from his post at
Seattle's University Presbyterian Church). Having just become
a Christian, I wondered what that had to do with the thirst for
success that drove me as a college student. I was troubled by the
thought that my degree wouldn't contribute anything to my
net worth. Since I was studying comparative literature, I should
have grasped that it was a moot point. Wealth, fame, and position
were probably not going to flow from my ability to discuss the
subtleties of Homer, Balzac, and Foucault. Nonetheless, situated
right in the middle of the 1980s economic boom, with its wave
of greed that spawned the term "yuppies," I wanted a few toys
and a nice title like everyone else I knew. Thankfully, learning
that success means being on the right road helped me, during a
formative chapter in my life, to avoid empty ambitions and to
direct myself toward something worth living for. Honestly, it's
been a struggle at times, but also entirely worthwhile.

True success is being on the right road. When the ancient Jewish
community wanted to talk about life, they employed the image of walking. To walk well in life meant you had found, and
stayed on, the path that leads to life and joy. This subsequently
became the Jewish concept of halakah, which derives from the
Hebrew root meaning "to go, to walk, or to travel." Halakah
directs not only religious practices and beliefs but numerous as-
pects of day-to-day existence. The well-known phrase from the
prophet Micah summarizes a life well lived by concluding with

the right kind of journey: "What does the Lord require of you, but to do justice, and to love kindness, and to walk humbly with your God?"

Being on the right road, having the right halakah, amounts to "blessedness" in the Hebrew Scriptures, and as far as I can tell, being blessed is a reasonably direct way of describing success. For example, the first psalm uses the image of walking, and begins by stating a categorical no on the way to defining the successful life:

Blessed are they who have not walked in the counsel of
   the wicked . . .
but meditate on God's way day and night.
They are like trees planted by streams of living water,
Which yield their fruit in its season, and their leaves do
   not wither.
In all that they do, they prosper.

The Old Testament is not bashful about promising that being on the right road leads to human flourishing. In this psalm (and other places throughout the Bible), it includes saying judicious nos to destructive paths.

True success is being on the right road. In the first century, Jesus— himself schooled in this Jewish wisdom—employed the definition of success we've just talked about. His vision of blessedness and success doesn't match the world's standards. Consider a few of what Jesus considers blessings from the Sermon on the Mount (using a popular contemporary edition of the Bible called *The Message*): It's when you are "at the end of your rope," you've "lost what is most dear," and "your commitment to God provokes persecution." Blessedness occurs when you don't have something: hope, love, security.

Is there an upside? Jesus reminded us that "the pure in heart" are blessed, are on the right road, and "they will see God"; that "peacemakers" are on the right road and "they will be called children of God." Jesus taught that being on the right road leads quite simply to *life*.

When you're on the right road—the way of true success—you prevail. This can be a litmus test for our goals: *Do they bring hope?* In Dante's poem *Inferno*, the following words are etched across the entranceway to hell: "Abandon all hope, you who enter here." Hell is hope abandoned. But when you're on the right road, hope is alive. You can make it through the humdrum life that most of us live. It's the kind of success that enables fathers and mothers to persevere in child raising even when it's all just changing diapers, waking in the middle of the night, and forgoing a load of personal goals for the sake of something greater, for the sake of nurturing a child. It's the path that energizes actors, dancers, and singers to keep schlepping to the next audition, to practice their craft when no audience is watching.

It also offers hope to those who are poor and will never achieve fame, wealth, and position. According to the worldly definition, they should be despairing because they have nothing of value. In the midst of writing this chapter, I spent a week with poor farmers in Honduras, in a tiny village called Brisas del Volcán, working alongside a team that provided a loan so that these peasants could own land and farm more effectively. We helped pick coffee. We built fences to protect their crops from wandering cows. We played soccer with the kids and drew pictures with them. Ultimately the goal of this relationship is that, through the loans and eventual ownership of their own land, these farmers could break the cycle of poverty where they make only enough to pay the farmer who owns the land that they farm. During the week, I would come home at night, huddle around a small lamp, and labor on this chapter, wondering what success meant to them. I realized they have fewer options for life. It's not a choice between college at Princeton or Berkeley. It's not "What kind of job do I want?" but "I'm thankful that I found work." Nevertheless, I'm convinced that being on the right road is still the way to success for them, too. In fact, and as weird as it sounds, they may have an advantage: Life in its harshness does not let them become stymied by the glitzy, fool's gold alternatives that surround me.

So that's the great yes of success. But this is about saying yes to no. What, then, are the nos? Let's consider each of the usual suspects of wealth, fame, and position. They indeed are good things. But they serve much better as perks than as goals themselves. They are penultimate and never ultimate. And one thing I've learned is never to settle for second best when the best is possible. To depend on fame, wealth, or position means that your self-worth and true success will be fragile. To depend on that trio will bring disappointment. Let's look at each of them in order to see why we want them and why they're not enough.

Fame has in it the seeds of something worthwhile: We want to affect the lives of others. But fame often only brings deeper dissatisfaction. The drive behind fame is that we want significance. So instead of seeking public adulation, it's better to begin with where we find significance, where we find what makes us more ourselves because true success begins with our passions and our motivations, not with the accolades. Albert Schweitzer, the Nobel Prize winner and twentieth-century humanitarian and doctor, summarized it so well: "Success is not the key to happiness.

Happiness is the key to success. If you love what you are do-ing, you will be successful." But even better than Schweitzer is what the Olympic runner Eric Liddell declared in the Academy Award–winning film *Chariots of Fire*: "God made me fast and when I run, I feel God's pleasure." And so I often ask myself, Where do I "run"? Where do I feel that deep pleasure?

But fame is unstable. What award will signify that you've arrived? An ardent materialist—a friend of a friend—was asked, "What would make you happy? Would it be winning a Nobel Prize?" "No, I'd know that someone else won two."

So the question comes to us: Does fame bring us what we want? Is significance really attained in achieving worldly suc-cess? Will a life of interviews on MTV and *The Colbert Report* really satisfy?

And then there's *wealth*. Yes, money pays for food and shel-ter, and that's essential. It can even buy a few niceties. I'm not advocating debilitating poverty. In fact, I'm not arguing against money at all. Having enough to cover the bills is good. Several studies have demonstrated that our happiness increases when our income increases sufficiently to meet basic needs, and also *decreases* as our income rises significantly above that point—when our wealth becomes high enough to bring with it money man-agers, a second house, and a dozen plasma TVs. In essence, I am arguing that wealth, by itself, deceives and disappoints as an *ultimate* goal.

The really difficult struggle for me is this: I grew up in a fairly affluent area—or at least a city *near* really wealthy people. I didn't have a church background to tell me my true worth is found in God's creation. Instead, money equaled success. The question, "Is he successful?" always meant "Is he rich?" When I became an adult, I gradually had to come to terms with whether my life constituted a success. I suppose it came to a head when, after eight years of graduate study and some serious soul-searching, I became a pastor. I've never gone hungry because of that decision, but it's certainly no way to build a stock portfolio that rivals Warren Buffett's. When I moved to New York I continually came into contact with people younger than I who were not working any harder, who hadn't spent more time in school, but who were making my yearly salary in a month or two.

Because of that struggle, I cling to my convictions about true success, because when I do, I find health and life.

You see, I've found this: What I really want is freedom, and I think wealth will bring that. In the end, however, money often just brings more money managers, more insurance, and more Visa card offers in the mail. We have a society built on the notion that success depends directly on your "net worth." That phrase alone should give us pause—that we are worth what we possess. But all too often our culture views wealth as a scorecard. But who sets the scoring? Are investment bankers really worth more than teachers? Professional athletes more than social workers? For one thing, working hard and engaging your best talents don't guarantee material reward. Even complete geniuses don't often make much. Back to Michelangelo for a moment, who grumbled about the times in which he lived: "Having seen, as I said, that the times are contrary to my art, I do not know if I have any hope of future salary." Instead, our net worth is what is left—the true form—after all has fallen away, chipped away by direction and discipline. It's what is "netted" by God's chiseling us through the good decisions we make and follow fearlessly.

And what about *position*? It does open doors. It's good to be respected and admired. So, if an impressive title comes, great. But realize that it's increasingly unstable the higher you climb. A

CEO once noted his title could be an acronym for "Career End-ing Opportunity." The pyramid is pretty pointy and small at the top. And that leads to the question, What is enough? What is the last step on the ladder?

In contrast, being on the right road offers a better guidance system. The commonsense dictionary definition of wealth, fame, and position is simply inadequate. And so many self-help books often mislead in guiding readers toward "success": "Define what you want, establish systems and disciplines to attain those goals. Go for it." Presto! Success. But it's like a rocket with no specific place to go. Start with fuel. Ignite the engines. Five, four, three, two, one. Blast off and watch it fly . . . somewhere . . . but cer-tainly nowhere in particular.

What does it look like to be on the right road? Let me recount my conversation with Tom about true success.

Tom, who holds a doctorate in industrial-organizational psy-chology, could easily be consulting for Fortune 500 companies in New York City, Chicago, or Silicon Valley, grabbing a goodly sum of cash. Instead, he chose the tranquil university town of Chico, California (where I also live now), about ninety miles north of Sacramento, a town best known for its Sierra Nevada Pale Ale and for having one of the top-five "party schools" in the United States. Put another way, Chico is a laid-back and fun-loving place. We discussed Tom's family's decision to radically simplify his life so as to move away from a commonsense defini-tion of success to something more personal. It went something like this:

"Greg, it's about mission alignment."

" 'Mission alignment,' right, Tom. I think I know what you mean, but can you tell me a little more?"

"We have a mission to become more simple and to enjoy the

value of our family. We sought to create a life in alignment with those values. So after a period of about six years, we moved from our upscale neighborhood in San Diego. Sure, our former house was plush and the paychecks were nice, but our life was neither family- nor community-centered. We had too little time for our kids, and our neighbors were always at work. So we never saw them. It was a paradox—we moved there to enjoy the luxuries of the 'good life,' but we had no time to enjoy them."

Our conversation continued, and Tom described their decision not to simply use the equity and buy a choice house in a more upscale neighborhood but to locate in Chapmantown, a poorer section in the flatlands, populated by a largely minority community. He clarified: "Here in Chapmantown, we find a richness of spirit. Our family has time together, and others have time for the community. Our mission to take time for family has been satisfied, and it's truly a win–win: The house we're renovating has helped beautify the neighborhood while creating economic value for us. But more importantly, we have a life full of family and time for community."

Yes, wealth, fame, and position are sometimes the by-products of success, and I'm not denying their benefits. But they can never be the goal. Why? They're like salt water; they make us thirsty for more. Success isn't about fame and fortune. Instead, it's being on the right road. And Tom knows that. He knows that to clear the path, we've got to say no—no to the standard definition of success.

So I'm going one step back: Use the power of no against all the common sirens of success, which by themselves—and as primary goals—lead only to the rocks. Listen instead to an inner voice, to the "inward voice one recognizes as wiser than one's own"—to the Spirit's voice in your lives. All philosophers and spiritual leaders worth their salt have emphasized that the worldly voices of success lead to confusion. What we need to do is tune out the static so that we can hear a clearer message.

One excellent by-product of being on the right road is that it allows you to focus your energy constructively. Still, it's tough sledding. So I have to tell myself: *Keep focusing.* Over several years, I've discerned that when I write, I "feel God's pleasure." (That's what I usually feel; other times it's just stress and frustration.) Focus represents a sine qua non for writers and speakers because it would be easy for this book or a talk never to be written. You see, one day doesn't really make a difference when it takes a few hundred to complete a book or an inspirational message. Today, it's "Why not just relax? Grab a cup of coffee, sit in the hot tub." The next time it's the demands of family life: "Can you just drive the kids to school this morning?" Or the kids: "Can you play three hours of Uno?" Or it's—in my profession— "Someone's in the hospital: Can you visit today?" You see, you can miss one day, but when you miss a bunch . . . well, it's bye-bye book. I love the line that I've discovered (but haven't found who gets the credit): "Some people dream of success . . . while others wake up and work hard at it."

How do you set your resolve? Guilt feelings cannot be the motivator. They are simply not effective and durable. They're usually formed by someone else's agenda for your life. Fear is another common motivator—fear of failing, fear of becoming poor, fear of being insignificant—but fear and creativity cannot coexist. The key to true success is that it carries with it creativity, hope, inspiration, and determination. I return then to those activities that locate "God's pleasure," where our deepest joys pour out. Those establish the right course. Then we are free, free from guilt and fear, free to be on the right road. Indeed freedom cannot exist without the power of no. Though no seems like the denial of liberty, it actually creates freedom: freedom to pursue our dreams, to live a meaningful life, and to reinforce our deepest values.

If you want true success, you need to know what's best for your life.

A relative of mine earns his living as a world-class expert in "branding"—the field that creates a lasting brand identity like Nike, Disney, or Coke. So when you see the Nike swoosh, you think victory, vitality, and sports. When you see Mickey Mouse, you think family entertainment, fun, and "the happiest place on earth." When you see the Coke mark and color, you think fun, celebration, and refreshment. I'm fascinated by how this happens, and so one afternoon I found myself in a car with this branding specialist driving around the roads near his home in France to pick up some good Burgundy for dinner. As we cruised past golden fields dotted with red poppies, I asked for his insights on developing a brand. "What's the key?" He replied quite distinctly, "Three words. A good brand must be described in just three words . . . certainly no more."

In branding, there are several so-called immutable laws, three of which are pertinent here: The first is named the Law of Contraction, that a brand becomes stronger when you narrow its focus. Two other laws are related: singularity, that the most important aspect of a brand is its single-mindedness; and consistency, a brand is not built overnight, and success is measured in decades, not years. So focus, single-mindedness, and durable resolve—those make a good brand, and all have the power of no embedded in them. After that conversation, I became captivated by the concept of applying branding on an individual level.

Here's what I thought: If huge, diverse multinational companies can brand effectively in just a trio of descriptors, why can't we? And, if you were to brand yourself, what would those three words be? How might this help create lasting success? At the end of the chapter, you can work through "An Exercise in Personal Branding" to discover what this means for you.

On the way there, let me offer a disclaimer: I do not endorse the element of branding that's just "spin"—that we create ourselves to be something for the market. I would be flatly contradicting myself to endorse branding as a way to produce fame and fortune. My use of the technique of branding represents something much more organic than that. My idea of "personal branding" often leads us to deal honestly, even brutally, with misperceptions, on the way to creating our best brand identity. Instead, I use this as a means to no what's truly important, to create a successful life. To learn to define just three descriptors for what is the yes to what is essentially me provides immense clarity in declaring nos.

One last thought: You might remember the scene from *City Slickers,* the 1991 movie where Mitch (Billy Crystal) takes two of his friends from New York City to a dude ranch for two weeks to herd steers and eventually they find themselves in the midst of their midlife crises. In a key sequence from the movie, Mitch decides that Curly (Jack Palance), the crusty old cowboy, possesses great insight and philosophical depth. (No one watching is quite sure why, incidentally.) One night, over a campfire out on the prairie, Mitch looks at Curly and poses the ultimate question, "What's the meaning of life?"

Curly extends his index finger with these words: "It's this."

"What? It's your finger?"

"No, it's the one thing. Once you know it, everything else is just junk." (I'm paraphrasing. He doesn't exactly use "junk.")

Mitch then gets insistent, "One thing? What's the one thing? Tell me what it is!"

Curly smiles and says, "That's what *you* have to figure out."

And so we do. It's only through saying judicious nos to the standard definition of success that we'll ever find out the deeper yes for us. Then we will find that we are on the right road. My own experience clearly demonstrates that it takes time to be quiet enough to hear a wiser voice that will guide us. But once the static is cleared, it's easier than we often imagine to hear that deeper yes. The next chapter takes this truth and focuses on caring for your spiritual life through simply switching off the technological chatter that surrounds us. On the way there, the following exercise, by using the power of no to create our personal brand identity, helps at identifying what is truly essential.

An Exercise in Personal Branding

This exercise is based on the idea that a good brand must be described in three words. Let's apply this principle to our personal lives.

Begin by brainstorming. Write out every adjective, verb, or noun you'd use to represent you or how others actually describe you. (I'm stretching the rules of branding that call only for how *others* portray you.) What are those words? Intelligent. Self-starter. Stubborn. Funny. Spiritual. Moody. Winsome. Ineffective. Dynamic. Energetic.

Then separate these words into two columns, one for words that you'd like to describe you and one for words that others use. In both columns, list positive words at the top and negative words at the bottom.

Take a moment to observe what you've written. What does this say about your aspirations for yourself? How do the two lists line up?

Assuming you have about twenty to thirty words, here comes the hard part. You start saying no. Remember that branding can use only three descriptors. Take a first whack at the list. Reduce your list to about ten words. Take time: sit with those for a few minutes. Then set them aside, and come back to them later. Maybe even tomorrow. When you do, prioritize them. Look for descriptors that apply not only today but also for your preferred future. What do you want to become? Let these priorities further narrow the list.

Three key words to define you should remain in the end. These are your "brand identity." Write these three words down for future reference.

Two pieces of advice: First, use a pencil so you can revise, and keep the entire original list. That way you can let yourself review and revise your list. Second, allow yourself to lament the descriptors you're not going to concentrate on. It's a hard truth that some dreams will in fact never be realized.

Read those three finalists. Meditate on them. Go back in a day or a week. You may want to make some changes. How does that "brand identity" really fit you? What will you do to deepen those characteristics? Do you need to make changes? What nos need to be stated now in order to realize this you?

CHAPTER THREE

Restricting Technology's Reach

In other centuries, human beings wanted to be saved, or improved, or freed, or educated. But in our century, they want to be entertained. The great fear is not of disease or death, but of boredom. A sense of time on our hands, a sense of nothing to do. A sense that we are not amused.

—ROBERT DONIGER, a character from Michael
Crichton's novel *Timeline*

————————————— • —————————————

I love music. And almost everything I've learned about the spiritual life, I've also discovered through drumming. Whether it's picking up or perfecting the quirky patterns of jazz, the scintillating rhythms of samba, or the driving pulse of rock, I've seen how nurturing the spirit and playing percussion mirror each other. Most of all, I've taken in the fact that growing in the spiritual life—as in musicianship—may appear to proceed by measurable and definable steps, but ultimately it's more qualitative than quantitative. Both spirituality and percussion need beating hearts. In fact, I believe the skill of "feeling time" is central to life because there may be nothing more basic than rhythm—the thump of our hearts, the rhythm of the day and of the seasons. Our bodies' cells even pulse to a circadian beat. They suck glucose, shoot out hormones, generate proteins and break down stale ones, all through predictable swells and troughs during the day. It's an inner body rhythm that may explain why we love music. Death happens when the rhythm stops. In another field, contemporary physicists are working at string theory, which describes an invisible world of ten-dimensional strings that vibrate at different pulses at the depth of reality. So rhythm may in fact be life itself.

The core of playing percussion is to internalize that rhythm, to feel time so you can learn how to express it unconsciously. Surprisingly, it's also about unplugging and listening in order to find deep rhythm. It takes time to feel time. It also takes time to undulate with the rhythms of the spirit. We as a culture have not learned how to hear the deeper rhythms of life. Why? One culprit is technology.

It's not that iPods, TiVo, cell phones, text messaging, and the Internet are the problems in themselves. A cell phone can save a life. The Internet can help poor farmers find reasonable prices for their food. Personally, I enjoy the way techie devices enhance my life and productivity. They give me music wherever I want it. They connect me to loved ones and they certainly can entertain. In some sense, they are truly "goods." Nevertheless, they can distract us and complicate our lives.

This is the central idea of this chapter: In order to cultivate a healthy, spiritual life, we must declare a no to the endless noise of devices around us.

But how, or how much, do we simplify? How do we free

ourselves from slavery to technology? *How do we learn not to serve technology but to let our techie toys serve us?* Here are ten ideas for nurturing your spiritual center by limiting the reach of technology.

Step One: Realize That Technology Can Obscure "the View of the Stars"

A gifted storyteller, the Danish philosopher Søren Kierkegaard illustrates the struggle between affluence and its accompanying technology, on the one hand, and the desire to "view the stars," on the other. This is a winning parable.

> When the prosperous man on a dark but starlit night drives comfortably in his carriage and has the lanterns lighted, aye, then he is safe, he fears no difficulty, he carries his light with him and it is not dark close around him; but precisely because he has the lanterns lighted, and has a strong light close to him, precisely for this reason he cannot see the stars, for his lights obscure the stars, which the poor peasant driving without the lights can see gloriously in the dark but starry night. So those deceived ones live in the temporal existence: either, occupied with the necessities of life, they are too busy to avail themselves of the view, or in the prosperity and good days they have—as it were lanterns lighted and close about them—everything is so satisfactory, so pleasant, so comfortable, but the view is lacking, the prospect, the view of the stars.

Many of us have become distracted by brilliant halogen lanterns, which too often obscure our view of the stars. I find myself in a thicket of technological devices multiplying around me, entertaining me, connecting me. Yet they're beginning to strangle me. And I wonder: What cricket sounds have I missed when I take a walk with an iPod strapped to me? Has my ability to see a crow or an owl become diminished by the hours I stare into a computer screen? Underneath the electric lamps, have I lost my view of the stars?

Step Two: Recognize That Ours Is an Age of Distraction

In order to succeed in this struggle between technology and our spiritual sanity, we must recognize a few key factors. Our culture is driven by sales mechanisms, by considerable forces of advertising and marketing, which encourage increasing consumption of goods to entertain and distract us. We face an amazing juggernaut that provides diverse substitutes for rest and true human interaction. There are antidotes for contemplation everywhere, maligning the very thought of silence. Our lives are busy, bleating with activity and noise. And so, in our buzzing age, we are almost never truly silent. We are wired for distraction, for sound, and for fractional attention to everything and everyone, but to nothing in particular.

One of my favorite times for reflection is when I am working out. For that reason, I prefer biking among northern California hills or running through pine and oak, alongside a rushing stream. Nevertheless, sometimes I'll head to a gym for a change of pace. But there, too, I want the same experience of peaceful exertion. I remember one summer vacation at Lake Tahoe— when I have an extravagance of hours to work out—looking forward to precious moments on the elliptical trainer, time for myself, time to feel blood pulsing through my veins, and time to think. Having suited up, I jumped on my mountain bike, riding to the gloriously appointed recreation center gym nestled among pine trees. After checking in, I grabbed a towel and luxuriated in the idea of some reflection while simultaneously toning my muscles.

The idea, however, was all I had. Walking down the stairs into the cardio room, I hit a severe disappointment: a bank of TVs was playing, stuffing the air with chatter. To intensify the insult: I might have been pacified by something worthwhile, some insight into contemporary life or the political and social world. At least a few highlights from ESPN Classic of the San Francisco 49ers with Jerry Rice and Joe Montana. Instead, that morning I heard an interview with the *dog trainer* from the movie *Men in Black II*! Given the vapid stares of the other exercisers around me, I think the question of whether to shut off the *Today* show sounded about as desirable as root canal. I looked away from the screens, used my Discman to escape into something just a bit more spiritually significant, and attempted to transcend the moment. (I'm not missing the irony of trading one entertaining technological device for another. But I digress . . .) I had conceded defeat, realizing that I should have biked not just to the rec center but *past* it and around the lake. And still the question lurks in my mind: Is this truly how we need to fill our free time?

I mean, it *ought* to be different. We *ought* to have more space, more time, and more leisure than our ancestors. For decades our society has been filled with the promise that time-saving devices would free us to luxuriate in lives of peacefulness, no longer having to slave like our poor ancestors. We *ought* to be lounging around, savoring what Anne Lamott calls "big, round hours." Could it be that we *want* to be harried and hassled and busy?

Step Three: Use the Power of No to Restrict Technology's Reach

It is apparent that we are more addicted to entertainment than previous generations. (It goes along with an affluent culture.) Nonetheless, there are similarities about the human condition throughout the centuries. We haven't really gone further than the insights of the seventeenth-century scientist and philosopher Blaise Pascal, who lived when modern science—and its promise of technological salvation—began to peer into our world. This brilliant scientist and devout Christian possessed such extraordinary sensitivity to human motivations that his four-hundred-year-old collection of reflections, *Pensées*, remains a perennial best seller. In it, Pascal offers this succinct and piercing assessment of our condition: "I have often said that the sole cause of human unhappiness is that we do not know how to stay quietly in a room."

That's a hauntingly accurate insight, and it suggests something worth attempting. Try sitting in a room. No TV. No stereo. No Internet. In a weird way, the lack of distractions is distracting. Our minds wander. We become twitchy and uncomfortable. So we seek distractions. Tellingly, in Pascal's own language, French, the word *distraction* means "separation, subtraction, absence of mind, inattention, heedlessness, diversion, hobby." And so we seek increasing amounts of hobbies to make us inattentive. One Microsoft executive coined a term for this state, "continuous partial attention." Or inattention. This drive is demonstrated most notably in the lives of the rich and famous—and for the hoi polloi, in our tremendous fascination with them. Pascal believed that this inherent, uncontrolled restlessness drove women and men toward wealth and worldly success:

That, in fact, is the main joy of being a king [insert rock star, CEO], because people are continually trying to divert him and procure him every kind of pleasure. A king is surrounded by people whose only thought is to divert him and stop him thinking about himself, because, king though he is, he becomes unhappy as soon as he thinks about himself.

I suspect that's one reason people want to win the Lotto: to seek distraction from their problems.

But at some point, the distractions cease and it's just you. With palpable wit and humor, Anne Lamott reviewed her life of addictions and obsessions as a means of battling "aloneness." Ultimately, she arrives at a diagnosis that is strikingly similar to Pascal's but with a different flavor. She tested all kinds of things to distract herself from aloneness "in sometimes suicidally vast quantities—alcohol, drugs, work, food, excitement, good deeds, popularity, men, exercise, and just rampant compulsion and obsession." For a while it seemed to work: "And I did pretty well, although I nearly died. But then recently that aloneness walked right into my house without knocking, sat down, and stayed a couple of weeks." I find this last image of aloneness staying with us provocative. There comes a point where we can no longer hide and no technological device can keep away the demons. We do all we can to avoid confronting aloneness . . . which is one reason we need real friendships. (That topic awaits a later chapter.)

Nevertheless, all these technological advances are fascinating, aren't they? And increasingly, they're just *cute*. Something so small and endearing can't be evil. The iPod shuffle is advertised for its tininess. Hardly bigger than a quarter. Up to 500 songs. Hangs on your back pocket.

Or pick a movie—the 1987 *Wall Street,* for example—and grok that behemoth mobile phone on the ear of Gordon Gekko (Michael Douglas). While "Greed is good" Gekko walks on the beach, he simultaneously controls the destiny of companies and gets a workout. Compare that device with the parody in 2001's *Zoolander* of the micro cell phone, which looks about the size and heft of a matchbook. Technology in its cuteness and ease insidiously wheedles its way into our lives.

It's also *new.* Embedded in our thinking is the idea that newer is better. So we trust in the recent, the fresh. And with technology, I'd be hard-pressed to defeat the contention that my previous laptop zipped through my programs and Web sites as quickly as the one I'm typing on right now. In 1954, the RAND Corporation proposed the look and size of a "home computer" in 2004. It was ten feet tall and twelve feet wide, and when you add the gargantuan dot matrix printer (and a steering wheel that looked like it was taken from *Gilligan's Island*'s SS *Minnow),* it would fill most of a small bedroom.

So what's the immediate conclusion? "Look how fast science and technology move—even quicker than we could expect." But God and all things spiritual seem, well, so *old* . . . and therefore inferior. I doubt we'd admit our bias that directly, but we might state that technology obviously progresses and religion just stays the same. So a technological prejudice lurks around our lives and can stifle spiritual health.

Now, as I've already confessed, I realize the difficulty of putting techie toys aside for me. I love gadgets. I don't think they're Satan with transistors and silicon chips. To have a portable device that carries hundreds of songs is still amazing. It almost achieves the category of "miracle." I'm old enough to remember the advent of the Walkman and how astounding that moment was as we snuck into the library and studied for finals, listening all the while to Toto and Hall and Oates. I like to make calls when I'm in my car. To be connected is to be productive. I live in a technological world. As I type this into my laptop, iTunes plays music downloaded from the Web onto the hard drive, my cell phone rests in my briefcase, and two e-mail accounts are retrieving messages (with an enormous quantity of spam).

So I find these gadgets really helpful. Despite how much I say yes to the power of no to weed out unnecessary elements in my life, I'm still reasonably busy. And I have a lot of tasks to attend to. If I can save some time through e-mail and cell phones, I may actually find some for activities I really enjoy. And technology can make me more productive, especially with all the options available for communication. I still marvel at e-mail and the wonder of sending the same document with efficient simultaneity to a committee in preparation for a meeting, and of checking in briefly with friends across massive distances without stamps, envelopes, and annoying time delays. When I arrive at work, my first thought is whether I've received any exciting e-mails. (Naturally, I'm not nearly as thrilled about spam.) It's a direct way to connect with hundreds of people. Office voice mail eliminates the problem of calling someone at 10:00 p.m. (which frankly is when I often have time to return calls). And I have a particular weakness for cell phones. I mean, my wife, Laura, could reach me on my cell even when I was biking home through Central Park.

And yet, to be honest, there's a downside: These alternatives often complicate instead of simplify our lives. The ease of communicating becomes a curse. At times I feel obligated to check messages on the e-mail accounts 24-7. Or iTunes doesn't load properly, and I spend two frustrating hours making sure I can download my next recording effortlessly. Laura and I spend a week of frustration and experience collateral marital damage trying to load Windows.

When I sit by myself, I'm challenged by silence, by inner desires and fears. I don't like quiet. It's disturbing. I want to be entertained. It's about fear. I'm afraid that deep down I'm missing something when I'm not plugging into the iPod or letting the music from my computer fill the air. I tremble at the thought of missing the up-to-the-minute Dow report or of having someone send an e-mail that doesn't get a response in thirty minutes or less. Will they think I'm inefficient? Will I miss out?

So, as a family, we have created a few guidelines to restrict technology's reach. We ignore the phone at dinner. We limit our kids' "screen time" (computers, TVs, iPods) during the day so that our lives aren't one continuous video feed (we find that a couple of hours a day is a good target). And, as yet, there is no Wii or Xbox in our house. A friend takes a weekly Sabbath from e-mail, and so we, too, have blackout hours from Entourage and Outlook. But most of all, we focus our restrictions on the boob tube.

Step Four: Turn Off Your TV . . . Most of the Time

Out of the assortment of devices in our lives, TV requires its own spotlight. Why? In 2006, the *New York Times* reported that the average American gazed at the Tube 1,548 hours, or—adjusting for sleep—ninety-seven days of the year. Yet how many of us complain that we lack time? Do we want to rescue some of those ninety-seven days this year, before they're gone forever? Let's grab the video controller and press the off switch. The power of no.

The time has come for me to divulge a family secret: We have committed the unthinkable in America. There is no satellite dish or cable feed in our house. Maybe I should be embarrassed, but we haven't subscribed to the best pathways for advertisers to stream into our home their clients' sugarcoated, sugar-based, and sugar-enriched (complete with indigestible food coloring) cereals, or Ginsu knives, or cleavage-enhancing bras, or Bow-flex, or any number of products we didn't know we needed.

Why? *We're not allowing ourselves to become the product that advertisers consume.* Here's what I mean. On a radio interview, a TV exec taught me something about television: "You might think that you the viewer are the client, and the show's the product." Yes, that's right. I was thinking that *Survivor* and *American Idol* are products I consume. "Well, that's not how the entertainment industry thinks about it—the client's the advertiser. The product is the viewers, and the show is simply the delivery system to bring together the advertiser's goods and the viewer's consumption." So I'm being delivered in my house to advertisers at my expense. Our conclusion? Not to spend $49.99 a month (plus installation) to become the product for untold advertisers.

Indeed we have also said no to spending our days and nights as a family in front of the TV. You may have seen the *Far Side* cartoon with a family sitting together on a couch, silently staring at a blank wall. The caption? "Life before television." How did we manage to spend time without the television? Did we really do nothing with those ninety-seven days a year before TV? We have taken time away from conversation, from family meals, from reading in order to fill our time with almost entirely mindless programs. Instead of a nutritious meal for the mind, we have filled ourselves with junk. Like junk food, most TV programs fail to strengthen us. They only fill us with an enormous pile of empty cathode-based calories. The power of no preserves time for what really matters, to commit ourselves to our goals, and to become purpose filled and successful . . . or at least to have a great family night together.

Step Five: Do Things You Love to Do

One of the best steps to a healthy spiritual rhythm is to remember what you love to do and to do it.

Help for our imprisonment by our techie toys can come from unexpected places. At least it did for me. I first really began to engage in this topic when I met Albert Borgmann. Professor Borgmann represents an unusual type of professional philosopher—the kind who brings together running in the mountains of Montana with analyzing Martin Heidegger's weighty (and largely incomprehensible) philosophical tome *Being and Time*. In March 2001, I was invited to a consultation with Borgmann on science, technology, and their effects on contemporary life. This bright-eyed, ebullient seventy-something man has developed a powerful concept, a "focal practice." What is it? "Focal" is derived from the Latin word for "hearth," the *focus,* in the Roman world, where the family met for cooking, for warming the house, for conversing. Today instead we punch in the numbers for the digital thermostat; my daughter codes the microwave for her quesadillas at 5:45, I "nuke" Lean Cuisine at 6:20, and my wife warms pasta at 6:40. *Why isn't it possible for us to eat together?* In the early days of TV, we at least used to sit together and watch Jackie Gleason in *The Honeymooners.* Now each member in a house has a separate monitor playing a different cable channel or DVD. Borgmann says that our technology—which we believe has simplified life so that we could spend time together—actually draws us apart. But focal practices draw us to our true selves. They draw us together. He counsels the use of focal practices with the question, "Would you rather be doing something else right now?" If so, you are not engaged in focal practices.

Borgmann continues: "Focal things require a practice to prosper within." His examples include music, gardening, long-distance running, and "the culture of the table" (meaning taking more time than simply nuking leftovers or driving up to Jack in the Box). These examples are often plain and inconspicuous, in contrast to the awe-inspiring things on which our ancestors were focused, such as temples and cathedrals. Borgmann adds a note of realism by acknowledging that technology seduces: "Countering technology through a practice is to take account of our susceptibility to technological distraction, and it is also to engage the peculiarly human strength of comprehension, i.e., the power to take in the world in its extent and significance and to respond through an enduring commitment." Translated: It's not easy to do. We resist. It's easy to plop down with our kids in front of a TV, call for pizza delivery, and watch *The Lord of the Rings* on DVD. And sometimes that's a great idea. But when technology single-handedly sets the agenda, we lose the key rhythms of life.

Saying yes to resisting technology directs us to the place where we realize our center.

Step Six: Center on the Center

Every day, I need to return to my spiritual center. Life can be distracting and demanding, and at times I begin to feel like I've got a jetpack strapped on, where I zoom through the day, bouncing from task to task, just hoping I don't hurt anyone. When I return to the center, I find direction, peace, and a humane pace.

Henri Nouwen remains one of the greatest spiritual writers

of the twentieth century, and he is a model of how to embody spiritual health. A professor at Notre Dame, Yale, and Harvard, a writer whose books sold millions of copies, a Catholic priest who appeared on Robert Schuller's national TV program, *Hour of Power,* sought out for spiritual advice by then First Lady Hillary Rodham Clinton, Nouwen largely eschewed the spotlight and found his greatest truth in caring for the severely disabled at L'Arche community in Canada. Away from the spotlight, he modeled the life of caring that is central to spiritual health.

David, a friend of mine, had the opportunity to talk with Nouwen during the final year of his life. No one at the time expected that 1996 would be Nouwen's final year (David himself died quite unexpectedly five years later). Sitting on a back porch during a New Jersey summer evening, David posed a simple question to this spiritual giant: "Henri, what is the key to the spiritual life?" Nouwen, with his hands moving from his solar plexus out, stated simply: "Live from the center. Live from the center."

I have since met others who knew Nouwen personally, and they point toward an inner restlessness in him. Henri Nouwen was not a perfect saint. And yet, in spite of his personal struggles, he knew the importance of this spiritual practice of returning to the center. In a brief reflection, he offered this warning: "A life without a lonely place, that is, a life without a quiet center, easily becomes destructive."

The need to nurture our spiritual lives is not something confined to Nouwen and other notables of the spiritual life. I once heard George Gallup Jr. talk on Americans' spiritual lives, and he reported that one in three people have had a transforming event that they can date—and that changed their lives forever. It's happened to me. But I've seen how I ignore those experiences. We all do. We forget how our lives were changed. And what about those mundane moments where we catch a child painting with utter self-forgetfulness, or glimpse the calm after a violent storm? I think these can all be exceedingly spiritual instances that can transform our lives. But if we don't return to the center, to peace and rest, we may rush right past them.

Step Seven: Open the Gift of Solitude

It's not just the lure of technology's buzz; it's the impossibility of concentration when we're connected to the Internet 24-7 or glued to the tube. As the contemporary rock band Switchfoot cries out:

> I'm a nervous wreck but I'll bet
> that that TV set
> tells us what we want to hear.

We need to disconnect and spend time alone. The psalmist writes with obvious contentment, "I have calmed and quieted my soul." But who does this? Nouwen, a natural extrovert, learned the value of solitude. And yet time alone is not all easy. He employed a striking image to describe this difficulty: "As soon as I decide to stay in solitude, confusing ideas, disturbing images, wild fantasies, and weird associations jump about in my mind like monkeys in a banana tree." In fact, he formulated this frustration into a moving prayer:

> Why, O Lord, is it so hard for me to keep my heart directed toward you? Do I keep wondering, in the center of my being, whether you will give me all I need if I just keep my eyes on you?
> Please accept my distractions, my fatigue, my irritations,

and my faithless wanderings. You know me more deeply and fully than I know myself. You love me with a greater love than I can love myself. You even offer me more than I desire. Look at me, see me in all my misery and inner confusion, and let me sense your presence in the midst of my turmoil.

So what does that mean about saying yes to no? Technology, which promised free time and peace, has torn us apart, and we have lost integration. We have forgotten to listen to the rhythm of our bodies and souls. We have taken on the incessant roar of the machines that surround us. Instead of living with healthy rhythms, we have only what the Grammy-winning pop duo Steely Dan described with utter succinctness: "I hear my insides, the mechanized hum of another world."

In the end we do not exist for ourselves. It would be tempting to think that this is about you and me in isolation. No. Solitude is not about self-centeredness or even about our private, internal spiritual lives, as important as they may be. Nouwen also re- minded his readers that the true nature of solitude leads us back into community.

Step Eight: Begin Each Day by Listening

How do we create a place of quiet? The greatest sages offer this advice: Take the first seconds of the day and center yourself. There the battle for your soul is fought. C. S. Lewis, the Oxford- educated twentieth-century writer whose books continue to be read by millions, put it this way in his book *Mere Christianity*: "It comes the very moment you wake up each morning. All your wishes and hopes for the day rush at you like wild animals. And the first job each morning consists in shoving them all back; in listening to that other voice, taking that other point of view, letting that other, larger, stronger, quieter life come flowing in."

So—and I know this isn't easy, believe me—take the first few moments of the day. Grab a coffee, look out a window or at a beautiful painting, and work through in your mind the day to come. Read something biblical or inspirational. Watch the sun rise. Remind yourself of what is most important today. Don't yet plug into the Internet, slap on your headphones, or fire up the TV. And if you have to rush off, commuting with the right music can become a time of spiritual power. Or maybe no music. And, if morning's not possible (like I found when my girls were small), find another slot in the day. Take your lunch break, plop on a bench at the end of the day. I remember sitting in one of those marvelous urban parks in the midst of Manhattan, watching and listening to the sounds of an artificial waterfall, tuning out the city's humming demands. Pay attention. Listen.

Step Nine: Learn to "Let It Be"

Too often we think of prayer as demanding from God what we want. *Give me, give me, give me.* If we say it enough, we'll get it. Instead, we can best understand prayer as paying attention. Again I turn to Kierkegaard. He phrased it perfectly: "A man prayed, and at first he thought the prayer was talking. But he became more and more quiet until in the end he realized that prayer is listening." After listening, we learn how little we control in life, and how to give ourselves to responding to what is.

Put another way, prayer means letting God be in charge of our lives. The most effective prayer for changing lives is "Thy Will Be Done." Ten years of scientific research by the Spindrift organization in Salem, Oregon, analyzed two forms of prayer: *directed* prayer, which attempts to "direct" the system (the rel-

evant slogan is "Make it happen"); and *nondirected* prayer, which
is open-ended and has no specific outcome in mind (in other
words, "Let it be"). Overall, the Spindrift study discovered that
both forms of prayer bring results, but that nondirected prayer is
more effective (people received desirable benefits), especially in
terms of what happens to those who do the praying (they experience deeper spiritual peace). We can draw the conclusion that
giving ourselves over to God is the most spiritually enriching.

Does learning to "let it be" mean we give up trying and
working? No. It means we've learned to listen. It means that we
realize that there are forces beyond our control. We release. And
we find strength to face life as it is, and not how we want it to
be. We learn what change we can effect. And we learn flexibility with the pushes and pulls of life. We move and sway to the
spirituality of samba.

Step Ten: Groove with the Spirituality of Samba

For many, time is little more than what the ancient Greeks called
chronos, the relentless march of hours and minutes and seconds.
Yet these clever Greeks had another word for time, *kairos,* the
"opportunity" or "occasion." *Kairos* is when time stands still and
eternity enters, when newlyweds—settling into their comfortable honeymoon bed-and-breakfast—enjoy the ecstatic bliss of
sexual union; when someone hears Handel's *Messiah,* and the
"Hallelujah" chorus pierces and elevates her spirit; when a new
acquaintance talks with you—over cappuccinos at your favorite café—and you realize you both love Howard Finster's folk
art, Steely Dan's lyrics, and Marilynne Robinson's literary style.
Kairos happens when the sun sets over an impossibly blue Pacific
Ocean and your toes sink into the luscious white softness of
Carmel Beach sand while you spy dolphins playing in the waves.

(It truly happens—I've been there.) You savor the present and realize it's distinctive. At that moment, you grasp the fullness of time. As the voice of Jewish spirituality in the twentieth century, Abraham Joshua Heschel, framed it: "Every hour is unique and the only one given at the moment, exclusive and endlessly precious." That's *kairos*—when the undulating experience of life flows with depth and intensity—when you grasp that the present moment is a unique gift.

At other times, what I've learned from music is that the life of *kairos* can be described as "the spirituality of samba." It's the samba's feel and sound that offer a musical analogy to the fullness of time. This amazing Brazilian rhythm feels something like the ocean flowing, wave after wave, on the beaches of Rio de Janeiro. But how do you create it? At a music conference, I took the opportunity to ask the world-class bass player Abraham Laboriel—who's recorded a host of those undulating sambas—about this mesmerizing rhythm. He brilliantly illustrated the nature of a pulse: "It's got to sound like an egg rolling." That's perfect. A samba is not an entirely round ball with even rotations. It's not a John Philip Sousa march that moves in mechanical order. It's oblong, requiring a little more effort to get over the ends. Each measure is a push-pull of rhythm. It needs a beating heart.

In the same way, mechanizing technology interferes with the spirituality of samba. When we become dependent on the technologies around us—used *by them* and not using them—we lose the samba; when each hour is managed and optimized, we lose the inefficient, but entirely riveting, egg shape of real, heart-beating human existence. A healthy life, on the other hand, lived with the groove of the samba, nurtures the spirit. So we need to search for God's rhythm in our rigid, clock-oriented technologically controlled world. How do we get into this groove?

We first learn to listen, to mute out the conflicting rhythms of technology that conflict with God's, and in the process we allow technology to serve *us*. And then we groove with God's samba.

In the next chapter, I take on four major problems that face us when we try to apply the power of no to our lives. They can be daunting, but they also can be overcome. First, however, let's look again at those ten steps that restrict technology's reach into our souls.

Ten Steps to Nurture the Spirit

1. Realize that technology can obscure "the view of the stars."
2. Recognize that ours is an age of distraction.
3. Use the power of no to restrict technology's reach.
4. Turn off your TV . . . most of the time.
5. Do things you love to do.
6. Center on the center.
7. Open the gift of solitude.
8. Begin each day by listening.
9. Learn to "let it be."
10. Groove with the spirituality of samba.

CHAPTER FOUR

The Problems of No

Problems cannot be solved at the same level of awareness
that created them.

—ALBERT EINSTEIN

———————————●———————————

I'm not one of those writers who avoid the word "problems." I don't rename them "obstacles" or "challenges." Problems aren't clumps of snow that dissolve under the warmth of linguistic alteration. No, our life journeys encounter rock-solid barriers that we can't run past, jump over, or swim around. They're just there, solid and imposing, thwarting our hopes and desires. So, if saying yes to no has sounded like a magic password, a way to zip into the Magic Kingdom without waiting in line, I have to be clear on this point: It's not that easy.

The key is to be aware of the four problems of no.

Problem 1: Becoming Dr. No

Some of the most common questions I hear when I talk about the power of no sound something like this:

"I don't like saying no. It's so negative. And I like to be positive."

"Won't saying no make me into a negative person?"

These questions are legitimate. Let's face it: "No" is not most people's favorite word. Actually, it's not my choice for Word of the Year either. And really it shouldn't be. If we like to declare no abundantly, we ought to be nervous. I for one don't want anyone to become "Dr. No" as a result of reading this book.

The anxiety probably stems from receiving nos in our lives. I've been there. In writing this chapter, I decided to make a test case on how it feels when someone says no to me. So I waited for an opportunity, which didn't take long. I asked a friend to help with a class I was teaching. He gave all the true and right affirmations ("I appreciate your asking me," "It sounds like an exciting opportunity"). But then, when he eventually declined my offer, my gut sank. Honestly, I just wanted him to say yes. Somewhere inside I wondered, *Why is he rejecting my good offer? Doesn't he like me?* Because almost any no seems like a rejection. And that just doesn't feel good.

The solution is to recognize that a no cannot stand alone. It must be surrounded by more vital and strategic values. If a healthy relationship between no and yes is in place, then we can remember *why* we say no and simultaneously declare no to the debilitating force of guilt in our lives. Nos must be spoken to things of lesser value to protect greater values. When we've clarified our values and taken time to be quiet to stay on track,

then we know the difference between what's merely demanding our attention and what's truly vital. Let me explain a little
further.

On the one hand, there are tasks almost every day that insist
on immediate attention and that also require a similarly rapid
response—when a child breaks an arm, or you realize it's the
twentieth of the month and the Visa payment's due tomorrow.
Those crises happen. And there's even a power of crisis they
evoke that galvanizes our resources. But there are also those
demands that bark for attention but are neither vital nor strategic, yet they tempt—and even energize—us by their urgency.
If we're not careful, focusing on responding to telephone calls,
instant messages, and e-mails can become our agenda—and we
won't have the time or the ability to concentrate on the tasks
we need to complete. Or we can become motivated by moving
from crisis to crisis and never arrive at more fundamental tasks.
Oddly, it's simultaneously a thrill and procrastination. Finally,
there is a category of activities that possesses no intrinsic urgency. Nevertheless, this third type is strategic and vital: financial planning, building new skills in your job, finishing *Say Yes
to No*, making sure you take that mountain bike ride to stay in
shape. These activities will never get done without the power of
no. If you skipped the chapter on true success, that's concerned
with defining this third type of activity.

The management guru Stephen Covey offers this insight
about no and how it keeps important things in focus: "Keep
in mind that you are always saying 'no' to something. If it isn't
to the apparent, urgent things in life, it is probably to the more
fundamental, highly important things. Even when the urgent
is good, the good can keep you from the best, keep you from
your unique contribution, if you let it." In other words, an unrestrained yes to urgent demands = a no to "fundamental, highly

important things" that create the center of who you are, of what you want to accomplish, and of the kinds of relationships you wish to have.

So know why you say no and you won't have to respond to every demand. That way you can say no and not become Dr. No. Saying no doesn't make you a negative person if it's meant to protect a yes or two.

With these values in place, I admit that it can still be difficult to say no. I've discovered this simple rule of thumb:

Say no with conviction but humanity.
Without conviction, it sounds like you don't mean it.
Without humanity, it's simply negativity.

One final, related idea: Stating your no sometimes means suggesting a substitute for Invaluable Me. It's the thought "If I don't, it won't . . ." If you feel genetically incapable of passing on an obligation, maybe it's that you've actually become addicted to feeling essential. In other words, we often say yes because we love the fantasy that we're irreplaceable. I find this particularly true of volunteer work. When you're asked to head up the sales for Girl Scout cookies, despite your amazing track record, it may not be the right decision. Don't say this: "If I don't help with cookie sales, the Girl Scouts will skid into financial ruin." Instead, try this: "No, I'm not able to do that this year. I'm finding I want to spend more time with my family, but I can recommend someone who can help." This is not passing the buck, but providing an alternative, while exercising your right to say no.

Problem 2: Those Who Don't Take No for an Answer

There are certain limits to the power of no. Sometimes a verbal no is not enough. Maybe the response is "Okay" and even "Sure!" but behind that word lurks the sneaking suspicion that the other party's not actually going to respect your limits. This experience brings to mind Ronald Reagan's rubric for nuclear negotiations: "Trust, but verify." And here I add, verify and regulate.

When you decide not to volunteer as manager of the Girl Scout cookie sales, make sure no one signs you up on the sly. And what do you do about those who "won't take no for an answer"—and even brag about it? It may mean simply repeating yourself calmly and consistently. (I'm reminded of the quip "What part of 'no' didn't you understand?") Remember that, short of force, most people have to take no for an answer. There are certainly times when a verbal no needs some heft, some body armor. The power of no does not substitute for a good lawyer or a restraining order.

Still, I've found that a verbal no is sufficient most of the time. So just say no.

Problem 3: Uncertainty About That Last No

This problem is certainly one of the toughest. The resistance to no comes not from outside but from our own core. And you can't shut the door to your inner voice. Every no implies a loss—when we're cutting out some possibilities, uncertainty and grief often crop up. We fear we'll miss out. And these are also times when the deeper reflection doesn't present any firm conclusions. So we sit with nagging uncertainty and second-guessing. Somebody tells us one opinion. Our hairdresser has another thought. How do we know what to think about that last no? Gather trusted advisers—people who have your best interests in mind—and pay attention. Have them listen to you and see if they hear what you're thinking. (And 95 percent of the time, don't listen to your hairstylist.) My own experience as a counselor has revealed a curious fact: The right decision almost always is already inside the counselee's head, and my job is not to give advice but to tease out that decision. In fact, that kind of decision is most often confirmed "in the gut."

Sometimes, even with a gut check, rank fear or cowardice prevents us from doing what we know is right. We need courage with our convictions. Indeed without it, everything I've written will become insubstantial—and in fact we will, too. As C. S. Lewis once reflected, "Courage is not simply one of the virtues, but the form of every virtue at the testing point." For example, you can't have integrity if you fear what others think. Courage hedges our convictions. If courage is lacking, nos—and the values they protect—mean very little.

There is, however, one more disconcerting experience. It's not what someone else prevents us from doing. It's not our own wavering. It's a huge Stonehenge-size pillar right smack in the middle of the road we mapped to our lives' great plans and ambitions.

Problem 4: When Life Says No

The final problem presents serious complications. What happens when you say yes to pursuing a dream but life says no, right back in your face? Maybe it's important to remind ourselves that we don't control all the dials. Often the circumstances of life take over, and so we have to admit we no longer maintain control of our lives' directions and the means of reaching our goals. Still, what we can direct is not those circumstances but our response. More important, I've found that these nos can present an exciting option: Are you ready for something you hadn't planned?

I begin with an inspiring example of using life's no to bring about a new, totally serendipitous direction.

It's 1990. Joanne, an avid reader, aged twenty-five, is commuting by train between Manchester and London, England. She's held various secretarial positions for the past six years but secretly dreams of working as a novelist. Constantly imagining stories does not help her job performance. In fact, in her own words, she's one of the most pathetic secretaries imaginable. Later she offered reasons why:

> Whatever job I had, I was always writing like crazy . . . I was never paying much attention in meetings because I was usually scribbling bits of my latest stories in the margins of the pad or thinking up names for my characters.

During today's long railway commute, characteristically she's reading and encounters her first problem: The train experiences a mechanical failure, and Joanne hears the announcement that it'll require four hours to fix. Today, however, she doesn't feel like reading. What does she do? She looks through the window and begins to focus on some cows grazing in a meadow in front of her. During those hours, the want-to-be author begins to imagine a whole new universe. Those bovine companions are the catalyst.

> I was sitting on the train, just staring out the window at some cows . . . When all of a sudden the idea for Harry just appeared in my mind's eye. I can't tell you why or what triggered it. But I saw the idea of Harry and the wiz-

ard school very plainly. I suddenly had this basic idea of a
boy who didn't know what he was.

At that moment, Joanne wants a pen and paper to sketch out
some notes. She has neither. Right then she could have stopped
and spent the afternoon in aggravation (which is what I would
have done). Instead, she finds the best solution. Using her only
available tool, imagination, she sketches out the characters and
plot of her novel in her mind. And, by the time the train stops at
King's Cross Station in London, she's conceived the basic premise for the Harry Potter series. By the way, it didn't entirely resemble the final product, but so what? She was on her way.

Nevertheless, Joanne's dream took several more years to realize. Her first book, *Harry Potter and the Sorcerer's Stone*, was
published in the U.S. in 1992. Joanne, a.k.a. J. K. Rowling,
subsequently won the Hugo Award, the Bram Stoker Award,
the Whitbread Award for Best Children's Book, a special com-
mendation for the Anne Spencer Lindbergh Prize, and a special
certificate for being a three-year winner of the Nestlé Smarties
Book Prize. (I'm not even sure what that is.) The Harry Potter
series has sold over a hundred million copies and has been translated into over fifty languages. Wow. All from four extra hours
on a stinky train and a few stupid cows in a field.

This story leads to a what-if. What if J. K. Rowling had decided that her life's no was the word of defeat? What if she heard
those cows murmuring, "Forget about your fantasy. Forget
about writing. Just sit in this train and wait"? (Actually, if she
heard the cows speaking, that would have been a different kind
of problem.) Nevertheless, *what if* that day's no had presented an
unanswerable dead end?

Or to phrase this concern differently: "Great, Greg, you've
told me all about no and how it leads to a truly successful life,

one filled with integrity, with health. It sounds to me like *blah, blah, blah.* You've got to realize that it's not always possible to say no to the demands of life. Sometimes life says no to you."

I know. In my life, I slowly realized that I couldn't triumph over the simple, daily demands of caring for small children in a no-resistant city with a pressure-cooker job. Sometimes life engulfs your nos. For you it may be illness, unrequited love, physical limitations, and other commitments, to name a few. But my discovery is that life's nos led me to reflect on this topic and change my life. Thus I wrote this book, which I hope will help others in realizing the kinds of lives they truly desire.

Thinking about nos that way does in fact change these mere problems into something more. I've gradually realized that just beyond life's nos, there often lies some new path. Now, don't get me wrong. I *hate* when life says no. I've read many self-help books. I've learned to "seek my dreams" and "never give up." I've learned to have faith that life's nos are often better than what I would choose. Nevertheless, there's nothing I can do about the roadblocks in these situations, and so I've learned to take these experiences as a call to stop and reorient.

So life has limitations, but even within those bounds we can still enjoy our dreams and the freedom to experience the fullness of life. Consider the sonnet. It's a poem with a specific rhyming structure of only fourteen lines. No more, no fewer. Yet, in the hands of a master such as the eighteenth-century English poet William Wordsworth, the sonnet became an art form with unusual potential, illustrating what the brilliant commentator Anne Fadiman called "the paradoxically liberating power of restriction." Within those precious lines, we are offered an amazing power of freedom—freedom to tackle issues of life and death, of love and loss. Within those few lines, poets grapple with all the major issues of life. Those constraints provide channels for creativity and freedom to flow. And sometimes life is a sonnet. It offers far fewer hours, skills, and dollars than we had expected. But within those precious few resources, we can still grasp what's truly important.

In the next chapter, I turn to some reflections on professional life and the power of no. It begins by saying no to relentless and even urgent work and recommends taking time to step back and consider what's truly important.

PART TWO

Work

CHAPTER FIVE

The Rhythms of No and
the Secret of Sabbath

All his life has he looked away . . . to the future,
to the horizon.
Never his mind on where he was, what he was doing.

—YODA, *The Empire Strikes Back*

———————————— • ————————————

The *New York Times* questioned a select group of executives about luxuries. The exact topic was this: Do female executives yearn for exotic cars as much as their male counterparts? The response from Andrea Jung, CEO of Avon, blew my socks off because she took the answer in a whole new direction. She didn't want a Ferrari or a Hummer or even material luxury in general. Instead, she identified an entirely different kind of indulgence: "Time. Right now, time is the only luxury I covet."

Time is the only luxury I covet. Would you say the same thing? Who among us doesn't want more time? Every one of us has 168 hours each week, but most of us haven't learned the secret of making time our friend. The key is simple. It's appreciating the hours, days, and years that we have by declaring no to the demands of our schedule. It's the secret of Sabbath:

> Don't work at least thirty minutes a day and take off an entire day a week.
> Say no to obligations and yes to rest and renewal.
> Take a regular Sabbath.

The term "Sabbath" evokes the deep springs of ancient wisdom running beneath this practice. By "Sabbath" I mean this: grabbing time to rest from obligation. On these Sabbaths we turn away from what we haven't yet attained to what we already have. More important, we cultivate gratitude, that beautiful secret of a happy life.

You see, I know the truth of Andrea Jung's response and the desire for just a bit more time to rest and renew. One July morning in 2001—just a few months after that epiphany in my doctor Molly Stephenson's office—I was in the final week of vacation, and Laura and I received a phone call we'll never forget. We found out that a friend our age, David—a pastor and father of two young children (the guy you met in Chapter Three)—had been driving along a foggy two-lane road to meet his family on vacation. His car was suddenly hit head-on, killing him and his father. His wife's first sight that next morning was not his smiling, vacationing face next to hers in bed but the face of a highway patrolman, standing next to her mother-in-law. Clearing the morning fog from her brain, she heard these words: "I'm sorry, ma'am, but your husband was driving last night and he had an accident . . ."

Then, just a few weeks later, there was September 11, when the complacency and comfort of the Pax Americana were shattered. That day Fifth Avenue Presbyterian Church—since it lies a few miles north of the attack—was in the pathway of those walking from the destruction of the World Trade Center at the south end of the island. The church's response? To open our doors, to welcome the confused and the hurting, and to hold prayer services throughout the day. Many who walked in those doors were still marked by the gray dust of the towers' collapse, some even bloodied, all disoriented. That day was tiring for me, but not without some satisfaction of having offered a place of rest in the midst of horror. In fact, I thankfully experienced only infrequent moments of personal terror. 9/11 brought out compassion and understanding among those I met. Generally, when I tell people—especially secular New Yorkers—about my profession, their response is often tepid. During those early months after 9/11, however, they'd reply, "I can imagine you're pretty busy right now." Still, understood or not, I was fatigued by the aftermath of that season. As I look back, I realize that I also carried subterranean fears and anxieties for months to come.

By the beginning of 2002, I found myself writing a sermon, "A Time for No," on the importance of Sabbath as a practice that provides space and renewal, especially for post-9/11 New Yorkers. I'm sure I was preaching to myself. Over the next years, I expanded those reflections into several other areas and eventually into this book. So, in many ways, this chapter represents the heart of *Say Yes to No*.

In 2002, I also received a grant from the Lilly Endowment that enabled me and my family to take an extended break by practicing Sabbath rhythms in our life together and by visiting various places of retreat. With various work pressures and the effects of 9/11 draining my energy, I was drawing from my personal energy capital, not just from accumulated interest, and so I welcomed an extended time of Sabbath. The plan: to study how western Europeans—who live in contemporary technological culture—take time away for rest and renewal. Following a particularly stressful year, it was perfectly timed.

During those weeks, Laura, Melanie, Elizabeth, and I took time to eat together, to worship together, and to play together. The grant enabled us to gaze on gorgeous Italian countryside, to walk the streets of Rome and sip a cappuccino as the sun set on the Pantheon, and later to meditate and pray as that same star's rays lit up the mysterious blue waters of Lake Tahoe. I felt the goodness of rest.

At one point, we worshipped with the Taizé community, a wonderful retreat center run by monks near Cluny in the Burgundian hillsides. The Taizé brothers had become famous for sheltering Jews during the Nazi era. Now they were more famous for providing spiritual shelter for those disenfranchised by the church. Hundreds, sometimes thousands of women and men, especially youths, worship three times a day, singing and praying to receive spiritual sustenance. They gather in a large concrete worship space, lit at the front by candles and decorated by assorted draperies, where they chant simple songs, punctuated by luxurious silence. Although the ages varied, I was struck most by the abundance of teenagers, expecting at any moment to hear, "Hey, dude, did you borrow my iPod?" These seekers come for a week or more, live in small communities, cook together, and study the Bible in groups. The overall impression was Sabbath rest, simple and focused.

A few days later found us on a pilgrimage to Assisi. We ascended the steep hills to the austere retreat cells above this enchanting medieval town where Saint Francis and his disciples taught. Soon after his conversion to a reasonably wild form of Christianity—one that featured his walking naked through the city streets proclaiming the need to sell all we have—Francis's message of radically following Jesus gained popularity. (Was it also due to the good saint's streaking?) The mushrooming crowds, however, quickly threatened his intimacy with God. These early Franciscans needed time to meditate, worship, and pray. So Francis and his followers sought a retreat in the Umbrian hills. I discerned there a model of renewal for me when my work became overtaxing, an example of the rhythm of activity and rest.

We visited various contemporary secular getaways. One was the stunning town of Positano, burrowed in the precarious cliffs of southern Italy's Amalfi coast. We settled into our blue beach chairs amid the hundreds of sun worshippers lying by the clear, impossibly azure seas. Some swam in the Mediterranean, others ate gelatos at beach cafés, and some others simply slept. We also found that families argue there just as heatedly as they do at home while watching *The Simpsons*. From Positano, we spied the island of Capri, where Tiberius, the first-century Roman emperor, moved the seat of Roman power to be among beauty so he could achieve rest and repose . . . and also hurtle his adversaries off Capri's cliffs at whim.

Our family also spent two nights at a castle on Lake Geneva converted to a hotel. We awoke and strolled out to tables set by the edge of the lake, where we ate breakfast as the mist rose and the brightness of the horizon melded with the pale blue of the lake. I was grateful for the beauty.

The time of Sabbath demonstrated my need for rest and renewal. It showed me how burned out I was and that the effects of 9/11 were not easily shaken off. It provided a stunning contrast to the shock I had experienced just months earlier. The contrast between September 2001 and summer 2002 was in fact so great that it forced me to go more deeply into my soul, which made my discoveries that summer even more poignant. They cluster around four basic convictions.

First, all these rest spots—in their wild variety—underscored the theme: *Human beings throughout time share a common need for rest and renewal.* There is longing in our very selves—our bodies and our souls—for tranquillity. The brilliant fourth- and early-fifth-century Saint Augustine considered his youthful wanderings and realized that he had spent his years running from the North African town of Hippo to Milan and finally to Rome searching for repose. Ultimately, his rest had to be found in another, more permanent location. In his *Confessions*, Augustine ruminated: "Lord, our hearts are restless until they rest in You." We are created for rest, and depending on our resources and depth of insight, we'll do all kinds of things to achieve it.

Second, money alone cannot buy peace and rest. Now, if someone from the Lilly Endowment reads that last sentence, I'm not saying the grant was worthless. I just realized that money—at best—can only create the conditions for Sabbath. Rest ultimately comes from a peaceful life and a calmed soul. One cool Manhattan fall morning, I talked with Jeff, a friend from my undergrad days at Berkeley who then went on to a combined law degree and M.B.A. He was practicing international law, consulting with Asian governments on developing energy plants. From the fact that he wears natty suits and stays at the St. Regis when he's in New York City, he's probably not collecting food stamps. I mean, he's rich. But here's the catch: Several times a week, he receives business calls from Asia at 2:00 a.m. Ergo he rarely sleeps through the night. And so here's this affluent friend, dining on the finest haute cuisine in New York, staying in four-star hotels, and his job doesn't let him sleep more than four hours at a time!

In fact, no matter how much or how little money you have, you can say yes to the luxury of time. Although rich and powerful people are often envied, they usually have the least disposable time. To become rich, most trade time for money. So did a friend, Susan, a young, vibrant investment banker. One week I asked why she looked particularly tired. She described her current client and replied that he had called at 7:00 a.m. on a Sunday. "Sue, why not just let the voice mail take it?" It seemed like a slam dunk. I figured that since she made lots of money, she could determine her own hours. She could sit on a beach and e-mail in her work. (I mean, that really happens—I saw it in a magazine ad.) I really wasn't ready for the response: "You've got to understand, Greg. When they pay you this much, they own you."

Making money does not in itself guarantee free time. That's why saying no to work can make for a priceless, healthy hedonism. It's beneficial for our bodies and our souls. It's also good news to a world of people who are frenetically busy, who long to see a different way of life, one that has rhythm and health.

Third, Sabbath begins the process of editing your life. I offer this analogy. As I write these words, I'm in the process of decorating a new house. On my shelf sits a thoughtful book on home design, by John Wheatman, voted one of America's top-ten designers by *House Beautiful.* His very first reflection is both profound and terse: "Edit what you have." What does this mean? "When I work on a space, I like to begin by culling the objects in it down to a group of essential items, each of which has a role in meeting the needs of the inhabitants and has found a place in the overall scheme of the household." What a perfect description of the work of Sabbath—to cull the things in our lives to what's essential and to determine how they fit into the overall scheme of our values and goals. Editing is tough work—removing that favorite beer stein from Oktoberfest from the mantel or realizing the 1970s brown velour love seat no longer works in the color scheme. It feels tough to let go and even like we're walking backward, but it's necessary for designing an attractive home and an excellent and beautiful life.

Finally, the goal of Sabbath is not idleness but a proper rhythm of work and rest. Besides being a pastor, I'm a drummer, and I've learned that great music is not just the notes but also the spaces between the notes. In some ways, it's how a musician handles not the notes but the spaces that makes the art. Notes without spaces equal undifferentiated noise. Space without notes produces boring silence. The proper relation between the two is magic. Similarly, Sabbath provides space. It is intended for us not to luxuriate in sloth but to create a livable, sustainable rhythm. Sabbath draws us back to the truth that our days and our weeks need work and rest.

One related coda here: Sadly, the grant probably came a little too late. By the time we were luxuriating along the shore of Lake Geneva, I felt overworked and brittle, a sponge too dry to soak up any water. When we arrived in Umbria, I had a feeling of deep fatigue, and not even five weeks away could refresh me. This reality struck me as surely tragic; yet it taught me that establishing a rhythm between work and rest cannot be rushed.

Gradually I've realized the lessons about Sabbath from this sabbatical specifically, from my own experience generally, but also from six wise voices. The first is Stephen Covey's, reminding me of a simple paradox: Rest is good for work. In his flagship book, *The 7 Habits of Highly Effective People*, Covey outlines practices that create people who are effective in producing what they want. He titles his seventh habit "Sharpen the Saw: Principles of Balanced Self-Renewal."

In other words, instead of sawing, sawing, sawing, letting the blade get gradually duller while our strain increases, we need to stop and sharpen the saw so our work will be more effective. (Covey's all about "effectiveness" after all.) Sharpening the saw is about renewing ourselves—physically, mentally, spiritually, and emotionally. Then our work is better—better conceived and better executed—when we take time for rest. For example, Sabbath creates self-discipline. And self-discipline is necessary for strength. On those days when we are able to put work aside, we can renew our souls. In a certain sense, Sabbath is the anti-workout for our souls. By doing no work, we create the fabulous ability to do our work better.

While pondering the positive benefits of Sabbath on the nine-hour plane ride from Rome to New York City, I ran across an *Inc.* magazine article, "RR: The Upside (of Downtime)." In it Kate Ludeman, a Santa Barbara–based executive coach, addressed the need for CEOs to take time away from their businesses: "I've often coached executives on the value of activities outside of work, not just to help them create a balanced life but also to help them unlock from their habitual ways of thinking to learn something new." Ludeman herself reserves time for riding a tandem bike with her husband, receiving Shiatsu treatment weekly, practicing Pilates twice a week, and meditating daily before work. A sidebar responds to the question "What's in It for Me?" with four phrases: "Finding yourself," "Relieving stress," "Enhancing your creativity," and "Starting fresh." Those indeed are the values of taking downtime.

At that moment, I remembered that the FAA does not allow pilots to fly every day of the week. They're required to take days off and to sleep so they'll be sufficiently rested. The reason? To make sure the passengers are safe. (It was a nice thought as I and the few hundred other people in that 757 were suspended thirty-nine thousand feet above the Atlantic Ocean.) My mind took the next step: What if we had businesses, hospitals, families, and government agencies guided not by overworked, overtired people but by those regularly refreshed by Sabbath? Would I get my driver's license faster at the DMV?

The third voice comes from Herbert Benson, associate professor at Harvard Medical School and renowned expert on the mind and wellness. He has given a clear description of why Sabbaths work from his research into the science of the brain. Dr. Benson calls moments of renewal "breakouts." Here's an example: You're sitting at your computer, pounding out what you hope will be a hot new book on, let's say, how to create boundaries so you can achieve your goals as well as health and peace. But you're stuck on one sentence, maybe even just one stinking word. You keep plugging away, but no word emerges. You don't know what to do because your publisher's deadline was in the last century. So you keep pushing. But the creativity never flows.

Using research from neuroscientists and brain mapping, Benson explains that up to a point, stress helps us to think better. Beyond that, however, it frustrates us. The key is to know when you've driven yourself beyond what's helpful. If you keep pushing yourself when you're at a dead end, your "primitive brain" (the deep core that drives basic functions and raw emotions) goes wild. That's when you feel fearful, angry, forgetful, frustrated, and so on. Benson warns: If you push on, you do it at your own risk. In other words, when you see these signs, it's time to switch gears.

So break out! Breathe deeply. Float in the pool. Beat a drum. Fold laundry. As the 12-steppers put it, "Let go and let God." Listen to U2 or Mozart. Countless possibilities emerge, many tailor-made for you. The key is to do something completely different. Then the stress function is relieved and creativity emerges.

Brain imaging suggests that deep meditation and creative activity lead to "coherence"—a synchronizing of the logical left brain with the intuitive right brain. There we enter into a cool Latin term, *vis medicatrix naturae,* or, loosely translated, "the power of natural healing."

How does this work? Benson and his colleagues suspect it's the release of nitric oxide that shuts down stress hormones and fires up those feel-good neurotransmitters like endorphins, soothing the struggling soul. (Just to be clear, that's *nitric*—not nitrous—oxide. It's also the chemical released by Viagra, but I won't go there.) Interestingly, the chemical formula for nitric oxide is NO. When you're stressed, let go and let NO.

Before there was Herbert Benson there was Tom Cootsona, my dad, and the fourth voice who used to utter a choice piece of wisdom: "Sometimes pounding more nails just makes more holes." Here's how I first heard it: My dad and I were fastening together two pieces of wood. We pounded in a couple of nails. The bond wasn't quite strong enough. So I got frustrated and whacked in a dozen more. It still didn't work. I tried bigger nails. It still didn't work. My dad said, "No more nails. Let's try something else." In other words, there comes a point when there are enough nails. Similarly, with our problems: We often try the same solution repeatedly. If a project gets stuck, we're tempted to work one more hour. "If I just work harder, I'll solve this!" But sometimes we don't need nails; we need a wood screw. We need to step back and gain perspective. That's the beauty of "breakout" Sabbaths: saying no to what's in front of you and yes to moments of rest and renewal. In those moments, we gain a fresh point of view, throw away the nails, and create a new solution.

Abraham Joshua Heschel, professor at New York's Jewish Theological Seminary, provides the fifth voice. Without exag-

geration, his writings supplied the framework for Jewish spirituality in the twentieth century. And they simply make a great
deal of sense. Heschel offered profound insights into the practice of Sabbath. (His life ultimately ended on the Sabbath, the
culmination of his week. Could there have been a more fitting
way to leave this world?) Listen to wisdom at its finest: "It is one
thing to race or be driven by the vicissitudes that menace life,
and another thing to stand still and to embrace the presence of
an eternal moment."

Saying no to work once a week had a social effect for the na-
tion of Israel. Heschel stated it succinctly: The Jews didn't just
keep the Sabbath. The Sabbath kept the Jews. Even when various invading powers (like the Babylonians, the Seleucids, and
the Romans) scoffed or even forced them to break this guideline
on pain of death, the Jews never forgot the fourth command-
ment: "Remember the Sabbath and keep it holy. Six days you
shall labor and do all your work, but the seventh day is a Sabbath
of the Lord, your God. You shall not work." The word "Sabbath"—or "Shabbat" in Hebrew—literally means both "seven"
and "to cease." On the *seventh* day, God commanded the Jewish
community to *cease* from what they had to do and to set a day
apart for worship, rest, and restoring the soul.

Heschel wrote, "Sabbath is an opportunity to mend our tat-
tered lives; to collect rather than to dissipate time." I see a culture
constantly working, striving to get somewhere, and forgetting
what's happening to our souls in the process. We squander our
hours and days and meanwhile lose our spirit. Consequently, we
need periods of rest to cultivate our souls. The Israeli politician
and Nobel laureate Shimon Peres reminds us that ancient Jewish
writers noted "the correlation between the Hebrew spelling of
the word rest *[nofesh]* and the word soul *[nefesh]*."

Incidentally, this insight is not restricted to Judaism. Siddhartha Gautama (a.k.a. Buddha) set aside regular periods for spiritual renewal away from his work's demands. Each year, as he gradually grew in fame, Buddha spent nine months in a grueling routine of public teaching and private counseling. During the three summer months of monsoons, he withdrew to renew himself. Similarly, when the seasons were drier and while teaching the growing crowds, he maintained a rhythm of withdrawing to meditate three times each day.

If it's good enough for Buddha and Heschel, it's good enough for me. It's also good enough for the best-selling novelist Anne Lamott, who continually combines humor, humanity, and profound spiritual insight in her work. She represents the sixth of these voices on Sabbath. As she instructed the graduating class of San Francisco Theological Seminary, "No is a complete sentence"—a truth for a minister and for anyone else. But how do you do it? She rounds out her remarks by saying:

Every time you say Yes, when you mean No, you abandon yourself a little; and eventually too much sand is going to leak out of your burlap sacks, and you're going to be operating out of a place of emptiness and deprivation and resentment. Whereas, when you say No, when you mean No, you create a little glade around you in which you can get the nourishment you need.

That indeed is the truth of Sabbath: to stop saying yes to every request that comes our way. Instead, in Sabbath, we create the clearing in which God can nourish our souls.

The fact that Sabbath might be more important than winning worldly approval forms the central struggle in *Chariots of Fire*, the film that won the Academy Award for best picture in 1982. (It competed, by the way, against the blockbuster *Raiders of the Lost Ark*—I'm still savoring the reality that sometimes the Oscars recognize films of this quality and spiritual depth.) In it the runner and future Scottish missionary Eric Liddell is set to win the hundred-meter race in the 1924 Olympic Games. In the film, the Olympic committee suddenly changes the qualifying race to a Sunday. Liddell, a very strict Presbyterian Sabbatarian, simply will not contradict his principles: He will not run on a day set apart for the Lord. Despite pressure by the English Olympic committee (he competed for England) and even by the presumptive future king of England, Liddell states clearly, "I'm not running." Instead, that day he preaches in a Paris church. Saying yes to no. It's worth adding that three days later, Liddell unexpectedly won the four-hundred-meter race.

Why does the story of Eric Liddell's refusal to compete on Sunday still strike us as inspiring and yet peculiar? Why is it compelling enough to provide the story for the best picture of 1981? *Because it's unbelievable that someone could believe in something stronger than worldly success. Because we'd all like to have that type of resolve. Because it might even make us excel in our skills.* As Lord Sutherland, president of the Olympic committee, affirms in the film after this decision, Liddell "is a true man of principle, and a true athlete. His speed is a mere extension of his life, his force. We sought to sever his running from himself."

I doubt that many who read *Say Yes to No* would decide not to take part in Olympic competition on a Sunday. But the question should still bother us: What will we stop doing in order to gain sanity and integrity?

I close with this: In 1998 the *New York Times Magazine* asked Leon Wieseltier, the literary editor of the *New Republic*, about a design symbol for his life. He pointed to his watch. The depth of his insights into our contemporary culture stunned me when

I first read them. He commented that the watch is "our punishment for the acceleration of life beyond the limits of real thought and real feeling, which must develop in duration. Instead we are slaves of immediacy." We too often push our biochemical nervous systems and our patient thought processes in this world of the mechanized hum of technology. And so Wieseltier, in language that evokes the power of no, concludes with this: "Thus my own fondest hope is to retard my existence, even at the risk of missing something." That phrase, "to retard my existence," summarizes the power with which Sabbath's no creates space in your schedule: space to breathe, space to return to human rhythms, space to return to your spiritual center, and space to find God.

The secret of staying focused, of accomplishing what's really central, is that simple no to what we "have to do." So, at some point each day, I take off my watch, retard my existence, and say no to work. I remember God and really live.

The next chapter helps us to say no by utilizing the art of improvisation. Improv demonstrates that form and flexibility together create beauty. On the way there, let me outline seven key practices for establishing effective daily and weekly Sabbaths.

Seven Sabbath Practices

How do you "do" Sabbath? Rabbi Heschel wrote, "The Sabbath itself is a sanctuary which we build, a sanctuary in time." How do you build this sanctuary in time? What are the elements? Which ones already exist in your life? For a Sabbath day, take these steps whole; for Sabbath mornings or lunchtimes, take them in smaller bits. You decide. This is all about freedom. We are free to discern what rest means for us. In that spirit, I offer these seven Sabbath commandments:

I. *Tailor-make your Sabbath.* These breaks have to be cut to fit you. If you're sedentary all day, maybe it's taking a day of biking or tennis. If you're screaming in the trading pits on Wall Street, maybe it's silence in a park. For busy parents of young children, it may mean spending time with adults. And if it's hard to free a day or a time for rest, send the kids to a friend's house or take a personal day when the kids are in school or day care. Whatever you do, just take a break.

II. *Let all of you be renewed—body, mind, soul, and spirit.* You can take Sabbath walks, lounge in your bed late on Saturday mornings, and savor Sabbath meals with friends. It's a wonderful fact that the tradition of Sabbath includes lovemaking. (You're wondering why I saved that piece of news until now.)

III. *Feed your soul.* Our culture is not very attuned to the spiritual life. I return to Heschel, who wrote that it takes only three things to create a sense of significant being: God, a soul, and a moment. The three are always present. This little word "no" has the power to bring the three together.

IV. *Eliminate all obligations; take off some time each day and one day each week.* No mopping, no cooking, no paying bills, no mowing the lawn, no fixing the house, nor even thinking about work and the office. Through it all, let your mind rest from obligations regularly each day.

V. *Restrict technology's reach.* Turn off the cell phone. Don't check the e-mail. And, by all means, unplug the TV. I've already covered this, but it's worth repeating.

VI. *Spend time with the ones you love.* This means friends, family, your spouse. Whomever. You choose. Pretty simple.

VII. *Reflect and adjust.* Find where there are things that break you down and where there are things that bring strength and peace. Adjust your life accordingly. My daily pattern combines physical exercise, meditation and prayer, and reading.

The Sabbath is time for me, God, and my family. Time for body and soul. Fridays I take the entire day off. Except in rare emergencies, I don't work. In the morning, I savor an extended workout, generous time for journaling, reflection, prayer, and study. I mountain bike with Laura. Sabbaths are days when I don't have any duties and everything's based on freedom. I even remove my watch so that it no longer breaks my day into disconnected units. Having practiced regular Sabbaths, I'll never go back.

CHAPTER SIX

Know the Changes
The Work of Improvisation

Improvisation, N: the art of thinking and performing
music simultaneously.

—*Grove Dictionary of Music*

———————————— • ————————————

I learned a secret about jazz from Miles Davis, Diana Krall, Steve Gadd, and Susan Muscarella, my first real combo teacher.

Know the changes
Master your instrument
Listen to others in the group
Then improvise

Here's what that means: When I first started improvising, I labored under the illusion that it meant being completely spontaneous, unstructured, and free. It signified "just playing what you feel." Thankfully—especially for the families that hired me for their wedding receptions—I quickly found out that jazz improv is not simply energetic chaos. It requires structure—for example, a rhythmic feel of bossa nova, straight-ahead, bebop, or mambo. It's the structure that determines rhythmically what good musicians can play.

Most important, jazz requires structured chords that offer the backbone of the tune. In jazz terminology, those are "the changes." For example, a blues song in the key of F generally follows a twelve-bar pattern: four bars on F, then four on B-flat, one on C, one on B-flat, then back to F for two bars. Then back around those twelve bars again—that's the blues. Only certain notes sound right when played over an F blues set of chord changes. Jazz improv also requires a dedication to the instrument, a commitment to skillfully play your "ax," that is, in the vernacular, your instrument. And finally, jazz is a community event, played out among the various members, creating a synergy that is (by definition) greater than any one member. When all those components come together—knowing the chord progression, mastering your instrument, listening to others in the group—you can think and perform music simultaneously. You create something of great beauty. You improvise.

In an important sense, work is jazz improvisation. Put more broadly, good preparation and brilliant spontaneity together make a beautiful life. From a commitment to structure and form, extemporaneous expression happens. That is to say, saying no to chaotic ineffectiveness while affirming spontaneous, creative effectiveness implies a yes to learning our skills, to listening to what's happening around us, and to creating plans. It also means a no to overcontrol, to the illusion that we can manipulate every variable—that we have our hand on every dial—and thus a yes to being in the moment and to the amazing interplay of life in all its dynamism.

Know the Changes

I've learned to thrive as a drummer by knowing the changes and by mastering the structure of the song. What is true in jazz also remains critical to succeeding in sports. In my earliest years, I played a lot of tennis. I spent summers in a white cotton hat, on hot asphalt courts, drinking from metal Wilson tennis ball cans filled with water with a tinge of tennis ball fuzz. That's not a bad existence for a California kid. I even managed to improve my overhead, collect a handful of trophies, and get a tan in the process . . . all before junior high.

Nevertheless, an ingredient of those years was failure, and here's the worst one I ever experienced. It wasn't breaking a string. Nor losing (although I racked up some disappointing losses, and I didn't necessarily savor those moments). It was this: I had a match to play four hours' drive away. My family knew the contest was at 11:00 a.m. So we all woke up early. My brother and I jumped into the brown vinyl bench seats of our Mercury Monterey, and my parents drove us to the match. I arrived a full twenty minutes early, waited until about fifteen minutes before—when players checked in with the tournament desk—and didn't see my opponent, all the while thinking smugly, "What's wrong with this guy? I guess it's time to tell the desk that I'm the winner because of a no-show." I arrived triumphantly at the desk with this information. Here's what I heard:

We already defaulted you. You're ninety minutes late.
Your match was at 9:30. I'm sorry.

I'm not sure I understand you. Are you saying I missed
   my match? I thought it was scheduled for 11:00.
Check the draw sheet. You'll see that the match was
   scheduled earlier.
Okay, I'll do that.

We consulted the draw sheet (which is the schedule of all the
matches in the tournament). Yes, the match was an hour and
a half earlier. "Check the draw sheet" subsequently became a
Cootsona family mantra to call us to be ready. We had painfully
realized the significance of preparation. (I was still a few years
away from learning it via jazz.)

Check the draw sheet. If the information is available, know
what's coming up. Figure out in advance how to respond to what
lies ahead. If you don't, you might drive four hours each way to
Clovis, California, and never play your tennis match.

Know the changes. Internalize what's coming. Life doesn't have
to be entirely random. *Preparation* is important and not something just for the tennis set. Unfortunately, I see many people
who have no plans and flit from one impulse to the next. And
with the power of no, I'm trying to help you circumvent un-
directed kinesis, the kind of very active but essentially unpro-
ductive life once described as zooming down the monotonous,
multilane Interstate 5 in central and Southern California surrounded by brown hills and thousands of cows: "You're moving
really fast, but it's not very interesting."

So know the changes. Each morning I like to look over the
flow of the day's work activities, meetings, and tasks and figure
out what I must accomplish and where the spaces are in the day. I
internalize the day's changes, offer a prayer for peace and strength,
and begin to play! I've found that once I'm in the midst of a day
in full gear, I know what to hold on to and what to let go of.

Incidentally, in this chapter, I'm focusing on managing your own professional performance, but the harmony of form and flexibility is also critical to managing others. If management is central to your work, you can apply the same principles with minor changes. For example, allow others to improvise through personal expression and the particularities of their skills and personalities but also offer structure—through clear guidelines and realizable objectives. Encourage them to hone their skills and respond to their environment. In this mode, you become the section leader in a big band, playing, but also setting the feel and sound for the saxes (for example). You're both a player and a leader.

Master Your Instrument

Jazz takes exceeding amounts of practice. That's another secret, hidden aspect of improvisation. In order to harmonize spontaneity with planning, an excellent musician continually spends years "in the woodshed." Incidentally, this phrase is associated with the "monster" (a positive expression in jazz) of bebop alto sax, Charlie Parker. He used to practice for days on end in—guess what?—a woodshed. Musicians woodshed as they dedicate themselves to their axes. I remember my first piano lesson with Susan Muscarella (after she had taught my combo how to play jazz). She had instructed me, "Learn all the scales on both hands, and then you can start on the piano." I arrived for the next week's lesson and knew about seven out of twelve on the right hand and one or two fewer on the left. She looked at me a little astonished and stopped the lesson right there. We couldn't go further unless I mastered every single scale. At that moment, I learned that despite how sweet Susan is, there would not be another lesson until I mastered those scales.

So competency allows for improvising. And that leads to the critical questions: Do you take the time to excel at the skills needed to improvise? Have you learned only half of the basic scales in your profession? How else do you expect to find the freedom to express your individual skills and passion?

Likewise, we master our instruments when we know our own particular style and makeup. Our lives are successful when we allow for "regional variation." Some need more form. Some need more flexibility. The pianist Bill Charlap, for example, is quite meticulous in preparation: He studies a song's history, who has played it and how, and how they've arranged the tune. Others desire more freedom to live "in the Now." Or, as Miles Davis expressed it, "I'll play it first and tell you what it's called later." In other words, he loved to flow with the moment. So to identify if you're a Miles Davis or a Bill Charlap, you need to take time to learn your particular voice. Either way, the key is to know your voice and play as well as you possibly can.

And Listen to Others in the Group

In jazz, improvisation sounds hip only in relation to what the rest of the group is doing. You might be playing the coolest trumpet run ever heard, but if it's during a pianissimo section of a soft ballad, it doesn't work. Over years of playing and hearing great music, I've learned that the best musicians always listen to one another. They make decisions as an ensemble. A quartet is first one before it's four. That's a secret element of improv. Work also takes place within a team, with other goals, aspirations, and competencies. Listening is indispensable.

What I've also discovered in my life is that the best parts of a day usually do not result because of planning. Instead, they can become *gifts*. And, in this sense, we "listen" to what the day is giving us. My mother even raised this to the level of a dictum: the best social events are those that aren't planned. It's when you've got the bottle of champagne already chilled, your friends are celebrating a new job, the sunset's going to be stunning, and you call with the invitation: "Hey, come over. Let's order out for pizza, stoke up the hot tub, drink some bubbly and celebrate!" That's a magical evening.

I'd like to take a slightly different angle on improvising our daily lives. My computer's thesaurus, by the way, offers "routine" as an alternative to "daily life." But our everyday work doesn't need to be routine or monotonous or dreary; instead, it can take the form of improvising, that is "thinking and performing simultaneously." For example, I hate to wait—which is really one big no to efficiency and my sense of time. But waiting seems endemic to work: waiting for meetings, for phone calls, for an appointment. Nevertheless, I've learned that with preparation, I can be flexible and even enjoy waiting.

I actually discovered this first at the doctor's office. It peeves me that when I go to the doctor's office, they're stocked with boatloads of magazines because they're planning on my waiting. But I've learned to see waiting as an unexpected gift of time, and I always try to bring a book, a pencil, and something to write notes on. Or I simply enjoy some time for reflection.

Similarly, I get bothered by interruptions at work. In my job as a pastor, my scheduled task to revise the budget is certainly less important than counseling a member in marital crisis, right? But the wife fatigued by daily fights with her spouse doesn't always call ahead to make an appointment; sometimes she just shows up. As I've noted a few chapters back, certain interruptions are useless diversions, plain and simple. Nonetheless, some are actually unexpected divine appointments. Henri Nouwen, the spiritual writer I've already mentioned, glowingly reframed this aspect of work for me: "My whole life I have been complaining that my work was constantly interrupted, until I discovered that my interruptions were my work." What work, what new connection, what new insight, can come through an interruption?

Then You Can Improvise

To counterpoint all this preparation and form, jazz needs *spontaneity*. Work also demands it. Our decisions necessitate it. As the legendary jazz guitarist Joe Pass phrased it: "If you hit a wrong note, then make it right by what you play afterwards." Not every note is played perfectly. And not every part is written out. So now I'm speaking to those who have just a slight control issue: We cannot expect our lives to play out in a predetermined, classical mode. There are simply too many factors that we would never be able to foresee and over which we have no control. I take this insight not only from jazz but also from the startling discoveries of quantum physics, which by the 1920s revolutionized contemporary science through emphasizing the openness of all physical systems, where one step necessarily and inexorably follows what precedes it. In the subatomic—or quantum—world, nothing is absolutely determined and predictable, only probable. You don't even know where something like a photon is until you measure it. Quantum theory threw out the clocklike, deterministic world of Isaac Newton's eighteenth-century physics with its precision and reliability and replaced it with an improvisational, open-ended universe. In other words, jazz now best describes our understanding of the physical world. And what science knows as the fundamental structure of nature corresponds to our individual lives. For those who crave order and control, it can appear all too open-ended, even a bit scary. Instead, with proper preparation, a workday can be a spontaneous and creative event. It can also quite often be exhilarating.

One More Once . . .

(That heading's a little homage to the great big-band leader Count Basie.)

So let me summarize by clearly connecting improv with the power of no. Jazz improvisation illustrates some keys to a successful life. First of all, say no to chaos: By mastering your instrument and knowing the changes. Say no to overplanning: Life is not fixed. You cannot predict every detail. Relax, stay loose, and take in what life gives. It might be a hidden gift. Finally, say yes to improvising a life of spontaneity, creativity, and beauty.

Having covered the secret of improvising, I will turn next to that critical, and often missing, element of character in work life—namely, integrity. This powerful and extraordinary quality emerges only when we declare no to compromise and stand for our core values.

Practicing Your Changes

I close this chapter with exercises to improve your improv.

- List your tasks for the day and for the week. Ask yourself, "Do these tasks define the way I spend my hours each day? Or when I review a day or week do I see a random variety of impulses?"
- Ask these questions and make adjustments: Do I want more structure or less? Is my style more aligned with preparation or living in the moment?

- Each day for four weeks, review the daily "chord changes." Adjust accordingly.

Finally, jazz is all about "training your ear," listening to jazz masters so that you can intuitively hear when the music "swings" (that's good) and when it doesn't. Ponder these quotations on jazz improvisation—and the ones embedded in the previous chapter—and discern which best fits your improvisational style. Then write down three to five ways you might change or deepen your daily life accordingly.

- "Learn everything, then forget it all."—Charlie Parker.
- "Music is your own experience, your thoughts, your wisdom. If you don't live it, it won't come out of your horn."—Count Basie.
- And then something a bit cryptic: "Don't play what's there, play what's not there."—Miles Davis.
- After pondering these quotations, complete this sentence in as many ways as possible: "My life could change or deepen in the following ways . . ." Then write out a list of your answers. Try to make it at least five sentences long.

CHAPTER SEVEN

Integrity
Do You No Who You Are?

This above all: to thine own self be true,
And it must follow, as the night the day,
Thou canst not then be false to any man.

—WILLIAM SHAKESPEARE

———————————•———————————

In 2002, *Time* magazine selected three Persons of the Year for one essential quality: integrity. This trio of women discovered irregularities, cover-ups, or outright fraud at their organizations and blew the whistle: Sherron Watkins of Enron, Cynthia Cooper of WorldCom, and Coleen Rowley of the FBI. On the surface, it seems that anyone respecting and promoting values like honesty and integrity ought to be rewarded. Yes, they did win Persons of the Year, but aside from that award, were they respected at their offices? No, in fact they received scant praise from coworkers. Some even hated them. Asked by

Time if they had been thanked by anyone at the top of their organizations, they all burst out in laughter. Their bosses decided to
cover up the problems. In a world of artifice and deception, their
characters had made them problems. I suppose that fact should
not surprise me (though it does); integrity is often devalued in
a world of duplicity.

Integrity: Institutions and individuals know its value. Its
capital grows incrementally. Nevertheless, one public scandal
can obliterate it. And one whistle-blower can point it out. A
Japanese proverb states this loss quite starkly: "The reputation
of a thousand years may be determined by the conduct of one
hour."

Integrity: Its value is immense, but it cannot be traded on the
open market. Maybe that's because it's beyond price. As soon as
we seek to convince others of our integrity, we've lost its essential spirit because integrity is fundamentally an issue of internal
character, whether for us individually or for corporations. No
amount of advertising produces integrity. (Actually, not everyone would agree. Some want to place a market value on integrity. In writing this chapter, I passed a realtor's sign today with
the slogan "Integrity Is Everything." Presumably that means
that integrity—as this real estate company defines it—will result
in better sales and thus the Almighty Dollar.)

What is integrity? Negatively, it's what you do when no one's
looking. Would you tell your wife that you had an affair if there
was no way she'd find out? How about a little flick of the pen
on your Form 1040 that decreases your income—does the IRS
have to know everything? Or for a writer and preacher, does
that brilliant line you're lifting directly from someone else need
footnoting or attribution?

Positively, integrity defines a life that's whole, that's *integrated*, where the outside matches the inside. It's "what you see is what you get." It's sincerity at work, which, according to some, has embedded in it an electrifying pair of Latin words, *sine*, meaning "without," and *cera*, meaning "wax." The story is this: When Roman statue makers found that their beautiful marble creations were chipped, they'd patch them quickly with wax instead of the real article. The process was easier and sounded like a great idea . . . until the hot Roman sun came out, the wax melted, and their shortcuts were evident. So the most highly prized marble sculpture was called *sine cera*, from which we get the word "sincere."

When we live with integrity, our lives are of one piece, not patched together with shallow values and commitments that melt under the hot sun of adversity.

The power of no guards and develops our integrity. And yet our contemporary culture runs on the caffeine of rapid change. Business gurus proclaim "flexibility" as a virtue, possibly even the sole virtue in today's marketplace. And, yes, it's good to be flexible, but that's not an ultimate virtue. Integrity and character imply constants. And we need constancy. We need direction. With so many options in today's world, we are tempted to be overly flexible and spineless. The path of integrity involves a no to worthless flexibility.

Let me unfold a few specifics.

Integrity means no lies to yourself or to anyone else.

Lying is corrosive. Then why do we lie? Why is it that an estimated 20 percent of executives applying for jobs falsify their résumés? Why do people act dishonestly at work? Here are some typical reasons.

1. *Expediency:* We believe that to meet a specific deadline or a performance goal, we must cut some corners. If that means the truth suffers, so be it.
2. *Peer pressure:* The core can be expressed in that lovely phrase "Everyone else is doing it." So who will notice or even care?
3. *Pressures from higher up:* Our bosses tell us to get the job done no matter what. Then there's that little matter of making money. So we'd like to keep our jobs.
4. *The ends justify the means:* The idea that the decision or act is in the individual's or the organization's best interest and thus would be okay in the eyes of others.
5. *"No one will ever know":* We imagine that the decision or act will never be discovered.
6. *Fear:* We tremble before authorities or before the consequences of the truth.

I think that last one may underlie all other reasons. Essentially, we lie because we fear the truth and its repercussions. And who's going to blame us? We live in a world in which lying on your résumé has become second nature, lying to a significant other is commonplace. I remember a conversation I overheard while waiting for a plane at Los Angeles International Airport. (Now, I want to let you know, I was quietly working on *Say Yes to No*, setting out my key values that I'd protect with integrity. The person I overheard was simply being loud.) This man told his friend, "I told her I wouldn't be able to make the event because of work. Of course it was a total lie, but I wanted to keep her happy." At that point, I was tempted to turn around with the retort: "How happy will she be when she discovers that you're blatantly lying!" (Thankfully, I kept quiet.)

Live a no to the corrupting influences of the World around us.

I hear you saying, "Greg, what's wrong with the world? I like the world. I enjoy my smartphone, my cutting-edge medical care, my Starbucks latte around the corner (and across the street from another Starbucks), my Big Mac, my five hundred satellite channels, and the energy of accelerated contemporary life." Well, I enjoy some of those things, too. (Actually, I might differ about Big Macs.) But I'm not talking about another angle on the environment in which we live. I'm talking about the World. (When you capitalize a word, it always sounds a little more august and impressive.) In this view, the World is not only the good stuff of creation, but all that good which has been twisted for evil purposes. The World takes the raw goods of life and uses them for more pernicious purposes. For example, the World takes food—to be eaten for our sustenance—and drains it of its nutritional value and inflates the price by adding coloring and preservatives. The World marks money not as a medium of exchange for our needs and a few pleasures but instead as that scorecard for determining our worth.

Think for a moment about the advertising and marketing culture around us. If you followed its siren calls, you'd be fat, in debt, and wishing for the rock-star life that you can't have. More important, you'd be discontent and lacking integrity. That's the problem with the World. It sells us short on what we really need.

In addition, all this marketing "spin" has led us to a deeper question of whether truth itself exists apart from the hype. Integrity replies with a resolute no to these gargantuan powers and declares that truth exists. Integrity stands for truth, not just for presentation.

In order to live with integrity, we must say no to living to please others.

Now let me waffle just a bit here: it's good to please those who uphold your values, as I'll unfold in the next chapter on friends. But here I'm emphasizing that with the power of no we find the deeper voice of excellence. That's the voice that needs to be heard and which becomes clearer the more we live with integrity. When we exist to please others, however, we create static in our lives that drowns out these more important voices.

I have a story that exemplifies this point. I only met the guy twice, but I'll never forget him. In the initial, brief encounter at my retail store, Top Spin Tennis, a "gentleman" paid with a check that had no printed address, drawn from funds in South America. I called the local bank, and they confirmed: "Yes, his account will be able to cover those funds." So I slipped the check into the register, wondering about my current planetary residence.

He arrived a second time, smoking a joint. (For those who weren't formed by California drug culture, that's a marijuana cigarette.) A fifty-something guy with a heavy German accent, he spoke loudly and with effusive spit as the by-product. Here was the essential dialogue.

"I don't care . . . I'm smoking a freakin' joint." (He didn't use the word "freakin'," by the way.)

"Uh, that's great. But I'll have to ask you to put it out."

"Okay. If you're so darn freakin' uptight, I'll put it out." (He didn't use "darn" either.)

"Well, I'm not uptight, but the Mill Valley police might be."

The man begrudgingly stepped outside and extinguished the doobie . . . in my flowerpots. He entered the shop again.

"Thanks for coming back, sir. How can I help you this time?"

"I think I'll do some freakin' shopping."

And then, to my amazement, he actually started shopping. First he went to the men's clothing rack.

"I'd like some tennis shorts. But I'm darn strong; I've got to get shorts that fit." He then bent his knee and flexed a tanned thigh. "Feel my thigh. Feel my freakin' thigh—it's so darn strong." He continued to tighten that thigh and pound it expressively with his fist.

"Thanks, sir. Would you like those shorts?"

"Freakin' yes."

"Well, let me ring up these goods."

My wife walked in as he was about to leave, and he flexed that thigh one more time for her. "Feel my freakin' thigh." And he hit it again with his fist.

"Yes, your thigh is firm, and here's your receipt. Thanks for coming in. Hope to see you again."

He left that sunny Marin County afternoon with rackets, clothes, and I suppose his marijuana paraphernalia in his pockets. But he never came back.

I have told that story hundreds of times. Every time, people ask me the same two questions and I reply: "I wish I could remember what else he did that day," and, "Yes, he really said those things." Behind the questions I sense the hint of a longing for the freedom of someone like the man in the store. Yes, I admit that his eyes burned with illicit drug use and his manner was manic, but still I learned something from him. Don't live to please others. Ultimately, live for that deeper voice that leads you to a truly excellent life.

What if we channeled that kind of freedom into worthwhile virtues? What if we declared a no every once in a while to pleasing people and being conventional? And what if we weren't afraid to say, "Feel my freakin' thigh"?

Say no to compromising your key values.

When we think of Michelangelo, or Mother Teresa, or Lance Armstrong, many of us feel immediate awe and respect. Why? Because they committed themselves to certain goals and they stuck to them.

I mentioned the film *Chariots of Fire* earlier. A quotation from it (as I recall) stands out: "Compromise is of the devil." The truth is that when we compromise, we give away a part of our character. And character is that something that travels with us. "Wherever you go, there you are." When we compromise, our lives become water jugs with a slow leak. Drip . . . drip . . . drip . . . And all that integrity has vanished.

Don't compromise. Say no. Guard the values that define you.

Jennifer, a relative who worked for a nonprofit agency, had a noteworthy experience. Her boss, the executive director, always felt a bit sheepish, and maybe a little afraid of the truth, about the actual level of donations (that is, income). So he doctored the receipts a little, even when he reported to the board: Instead of $14,500 this month, it was $20,000. Instead of a year-to-date deficit of $53,000, it was $40,000. I mean, I remember arithmetic, and this isn't even rounding the numbers! The problem for Jen was that she was the development director, and you can't raise funds effectively when you don't know what's really coming in. But why did the executive director stretch the truth and stretch his integrity in the process? Because he dreaded what might happen if people really knew the story. Ironically, the truth might have motivated potential donors to give or energized the board to engage in fund-raising.

Just make it a habit not to lie and you never will. When you try, it won't work. (This may be a problem when you want to plan a surprise party, but it's worth it.) In the process of learn-ing how to be a bad liar, you'll have saved yourself from the crumbling effects of lying. This process can even be humorous. What if, for one single day, we couldn't lie? My friend Paul Guay co-wrote the script for the comedy film *Liar Liar*. The essential premise is that the fast-track lawyer Fletcher Reede can't lie for twenty-four hours because his son made a birthday wish after Reede let him down for the last time. A lawyer who can't lie makes for good comedy. Here's an interchange in the courtroom:

> Judge Stevens: Mr. Reede, one more word out of you,
> and I will hold you in contempt!
> Fletcher: I hold myself in contempt! Why should you be
> any different?

Paul is onto something. When we lie and compromise our integrity, we risk finding ourselves contemptible.

Sometimes integrity means forging ahead when those in authority dis-courage us.

Integrity demands that we don't slavishly follow our men-tors.

Consider the famous philosopher Aristotle describing his dif-ferences from his mentor: "I love Plato, and I love the truth. But I love truth more." And I love that quotation. Because some-times integrity means acknowledging differences and standing by them, letting your teachers know you care more about the values you both hold to—like truth—than about their specific conclusions. And every once in a while, teachers disappoint. I hope we do love the truth more than any one person.

Integrity: No who you are.

It's worth the effort. It's a gift to yourself because nothing, not hardship, nor poverty, nor disability, can take it away. It's also really a gift to others and to our culture of spin, where truth seems to be in short supply. It's a gift that's beyond price.

Having brought the power of no to bear on three key areas of work, I begin Part Three, in which I discuss relationships and saying no so that we can develop healthy friendships, families, and marriages. When we say the right nos in our relationships, we say yes to the good life.

Developing Deeper Integrity

1. Identify your solid values. What components of the world threaten those values? When and where is your integrity tested? How might you avoid those situations? Make a chart for yourself that lists your core values, the threats to your values, and the responses you might have ready for these threats.

2. Find those close friends who will help you sustain these values. E-mail or call. Maybe sit down with them over lunch or coffee. Let them know you want to develop and maintain these values. Elicit their help in becoming a person of integrity.

3. Write out a brief statement of your core values, the threats to them, and your response. Set your calendar to remind yourself twice a year to review them.

PART THREE

Love

CHAPTER EIGHT

No to a Lonely Life

God evidently does not intend us all to be rich, or powerful
or great, but He does intend us all to be friends.

—RALPH WALDO EMERSON, nineteenth-century
American philosopher and writer

———————●———————

Two respected observers offer some disturbing news about community life in the United States. The first, the Harvard sociologist Robert Putnam, analyzed American lifestyles. Dr. Putnam discovered that our emphasis on personal freedom and individual expression often means we live separated from one another. Our country has squandered a key value, "social capital"—the bank of social trust, norms, and networks that people draw on to solve common problems—exchanging it for individualism, self-expression, and autonomy.

Social capital requires strong cohesion within society. As

Putnam studied bowling habits over the past few decades (yes, *bowling* habits), he discovered that this sport indicates a great deal about American life. As a culture, we now bowl more frequently. Nevertheless, we used to bowl primarily in leagues—in other words, in community—and now it's a solitary activity. We hit the local lanes more than we did thirty years ago, but we do it by ourselves. To quote Putnam's pithy phrase—and the title of his book—we often find ourselves "bowling alone."

Similarly, George Gallup Jr., the widely acclaimed pollster and commentator on life in the United States, reports that "Americans are perhaps the loneliest people on earth today." He suggests that we suffer from "personal isolationism." This takes a serious toll on our well-being, both socially and spiritually. Experiencing isolation can lead to feelings of hostility, anger, exhaustion, and depression. Human beings are not meant to live this way. Without relationships, we find only despair. To cite the famous Russian novelist Fyodor Dostoyevsky, "Hell is the suffering of being unable to love."

In fact, scientific research has reinforced Gallup's conclusions. For many years, I've followed, and participated in, a dialogue about religion and science. I'm currently directing a three-year project called the Chico Triad on Philosophy, Theology, and Science which brings together scholars in physics, biblical studies, psychology, religious studies, logic, theology, metaphysics, and chemistry. We have a fabulous time together, discussing, arguing, and discovering how these diverse fields interact. One core issue we continue returning to is human nature and the enduring need human beings have—psychologically, biologically, theologically, ethically—to relate to one another. We've discovered some key insights that resonate with a conference that took place a few years ago in New York City. The topic?

The human being. Scientists and theologians sought to determine what it really means to be human. The biblical scholars reminded those assembled that Jewish and Christian Scriptures teach the need to make human connections, that in fact the book of Genesis calls this "the image of God." Neuroscientists and psychologists brought contemporary research that analyzed the psychology and brain function of humans. What did these eminent minds conclude? "Relationality"—the ability and need to relate to another—forms a critical component of being human. Subsequently, I've read in several journals that relating positively toward others—that is, loving and respecting others—is critical for good mental and physical health. We are created to relate. We are created to love.

Here's a basic exercise. Think back over your life. What are the times that stand out? I'll bet that 90 percent or more of those significant memories involve relationships. I know when I've looked over my life, the truly important components always orbit around friendships—Laura and our first date on January 1, 1981; the times I spent with my daughters at Lake Tahoe; Brian and Lincoln, the pianist and alto saxophonist in my first jazz combo during college; Steve and Jon, my friends in graduate school in Princeton; my mom and dad camping with me and my brother at Lake Tahoe. Why? Because there I shared life with people whom I loved and who loved me. Maybe the Beatles were right when they sang, "All you need is love." Or, at least without love, everything else is pretty empty.

We are made for relationships. We are not really even ourselves unless we have friends and unless we serve others. The potency of friendship—a value, I feel, too few Americans know—is a gift that depends on saying yes to no. Say no to loneliness and selfishness and find the power of friendship.

_____

Let's move, then, to a definition of love.

If we don't grasp accurately the nature of love, then we can go nowhere. Friendship is where we understand the nature of love because generally we choose our friends and therefore we choose to love them. So let me define love.

But first I admit there's a problem: The definitions of love that fill the airwaves and our DVDs portray erotic love—that spontaneous, overwhelming surge of passion. This sort of love (not at all to be devalued) is a powerful feeling. It's beautiful, and amazing, and even a gift of God. It juices us full of biochemical elation. (And it sells a lot of products out there.) But that's not what I mean by love—certainly not at its core. It's not even what creates a great marriage (which I'll cover in Chapter Ten).

Instead of overwhelming emotion, here's the indispensable definition: *Love is actively willing and working for another's best.* This destroys at least two myths. First: Love is not simply—and even primarily—an emotion. Love is an action and involves both "willing and working." But it is also not sentimental hash. C. S. Lewis, who keeps reappearing in this book, reminded me that love is not about soft, generalized kindness that pronounces, "What does it matter as long as they're happy?" Kindness is a component of love, but they are not the same. "Kindness," Lewis writes, "merely as such, cares not whether its object becomes good or bad, provided only that it escapes suffering." Sometimes love leads us to say the hard word that hurts because it's true and it will lead our friends to be their best.

Positive, loving relationships are so central that as human beings, *we don't even realize our own particular talents until we let others in.* Consider the case of J. R. R. Tolkien, whose *Lord of the Rings* remains one of the enduring classic books of our time. In fact, a

1999 Amazon.com customers' poll chose *Lord of the Rings* as the greatest book not just of a mere century but of the millennium. In case you've missed the hype, this fantasy trilogy concerns the small-fry hobbit (a "halfing") Frodo and his friend Sam, who set out to save their world from great evil by destroying the One Ring of Power, created by the evil Lord Sauron to enslave all beings. Tolkien began the mythology for this story in the foxholes of France as a soldier in World War I. As a professor of English literature *(Old* English—*Beowulf,* that kind of thing), Tolkien was never a full-time writer, but he gradually and on the side created his own legendary world of elves, dwarfs, wizards, and orcs. The entire process took almost four decades until the books began being published in 1954. Then, another four decades later, the filmmaker and director Peter Jackson himself embarked on an eight-year odyssey to produce his cinematic trilogy. Completed in 2003, the final installment, *The Return of the King,* alone won eleven Academy Awards, including best picture and best director.

A fabulous story. But did you realize that the trilogy almost never got published in the first place? Tolkien constantly toiled over the work. He frequently hit snags in creating his story. At one point, the wizard Gandalf plunges down the cavernous, dank, and dangerous Mines of Moria, and Tolkien didn't know how to complete the narrative. He broke off writing for an entire year. During this time, he was reading his work to a small group of Oxford intellectual lights called the Inklings, which included Charles Williams ("C.W." below) and C. S. Lewis ("C.S.L."). Listen to the description of his struggles in a letter he wrote to his son Christopher Tolkien:

> I worked very hard at my chapter—it is very exhausting work; especially as the climax approaches and one has to

keep the pitch up: no easy level will do; and there are all sorts of minor problems of plot and mechanism. I wrote and tore up and rewrote most of it a good many times; but I was rewarded this morning as both C.S.L. and C.W. thought it an admirable performance and the latest chapters the best so far.

These two Inklings, Lewis and Williams, provided constant support, and inspiration, to Tolkien. In light of his frequent anxiety that no one would actually enjoy his meandering mythology, Tolkien later described the distinctive influence of C. S. Lewis: "The unpayable debt that I owe to him was not 'influence' as it is ordinarily understood, but sheer encouragement. He was for long my only audience. Only from him did I ever get the idea that my 'stuff' could be more than a private hobby." That phrase, "a private hobby," astounds me because that "hobby" became the book of the millennium! And the story behind the story is the power of friendship and how it motivates and enhances our lives. Friends, at their best, help us move forward. We, of course, are probably not secretly concocting the best novel of the next one thousand years. Still, we have to ask, how many "private hobbies" do we have that are currently buried but simply need a friend's encouragement?

Friendship kindles confidence. Even more, it assists us in finding our true selves. This fact cuts against the grain of a long-standing temptation in Western society to assert that our self-understanding comes from individual effort. The seventeenth-century philosopher René Descartes usually receives the blame for getting this started. Within his famous room for reflection—heated high enough that he named it "The Oven"—Descartes declared the famous aphorism "I think, therefore I am." My emphasis here falls on Descartes doing this thinking by himself, determining his existence (his "I-am-ness") without anyone else around. If that just seems a little French for some readers, try the American Henry Thoreau, who two centuries later cloistered himself at Walden Pond. There, by himself, he reflected on his existence and "found himself" (to use 1960s jargon). For Thoreau, life was all about bliss, truth, and presumably cheap rent.

Unlike Descartes and Thoreau, I learned that we don't find truth alone; we find it in community. We aren't really ourselves unless we have friends. Sadly, according to Gallup and Putnam, the idea of community and friendship is gradually slipping from our grasp.

But we have to hold on. How do we begin? Below I'll describe six applications of the power of no to help you enjoy the fullness of friendship.

First of all, friends spend time together, and that means saying no to quantity over quality.

Does it sound like this all comes down to time? In many ways, yes, that's the basis of good relationships. I suppose here we have to fight the American temptation of "fast food" friendships, delivered quickly and disposed of when they are no longer needed. We also will need to counter the common assertion that all we need is "quality time" (as if that exists without quantity of time). Anything of value—a book, a symphony, a flower, a relationship—takes time to develop. Good friendships rarely happen immediately; instead, they, like genuine thought and feeling, need nourishing.

Furthermore, we can't have innumerable friends. Sociological studies suggest that we can take on perhaps five to seven truly significant relationships. (Apparently, this number relates to our early needs for survival; if you have half a dozen watching your back, you're more likely to survive.) That's your core group—that's what the rap stars call your "posse" or your "crew." (I'm trying to be hip here.) Intention is critical because time is critical. So we need to determine who those essential half-dozen friends are and take time to develop those relationships.

In addition, relationships need conversation, which means a no to one-sided talking and a yes to listening.

Real dialogue means opening ourselves to others. And in good conversation we let go of our need to control. We listen. One of the elements of true interactive talking is that you let go—let go of what *you'd* like the other person to say and let him or her express what's inside. There is the old proverb, "We are given two ears and one mouth and ought to use them in that proportion." When we listen, we open ourselves up and allow space for others to grow. Here's a simple test: Can you repeat the substance of what your friend is saying? If so, you're really listening.

And this is the right place to add that another no emerges from listening. We can't live armed with preemptive nos—foregone negations of what we suspect others will say (and indeed what they do repeatedly say). Instead, listening means we set aside our prefabricated responses long enough to hear any new information.

Friendship implies disagreement: this means a no to forced consensus.

Let's imagine you're driving with a friend. She asks a simple question about your thoughts on politics. She asserts that Lithuania is the next emerging superpower. You express some hesitation. She responds with stinging and significant criticisms. How will you feel? If you're smart, you'll realize that you can never disagree with her about politics and that there may be other, as yet undiscussed areas that are off-limits. But she's missed an opportunity because conflict, oddly enough, can lead to intimacy if we engage it sensitively. If I know what really angers you, I know what's most important to you.

In the United States, we are not particularly good at handling disputes. I think this stems from the mobility of our culture (we can "blow off" a relationship because there's a good chance that person may move away in a few years) and that increasingly the majority of people do not subscribe to unselfish values and humanistic cultural norms (that is, our social capital is decreasing). Let's see if I can illustrate this: When my wife, Laura, first arrived in Italy as a high-school exchange student, she was astonished on the first night with her host family; there could be fierce argument during the pasta course and then laughter by the time the veal piccata was served. But here's the key: *They knew they'd be together after the interchange for years to come. They had to work it out.*

My experience in leadership is that this principle applies equally to work environments. It may not seem to make sense at first, but good disagreement fosters and sustains real collaborative work. In fact, I've discovered that true conflict is intimate because when we disagree, we learn what really matters. We know who we're actually working with. But this also implies a commitment to stay together.

This brings me to a coda about professional relationships and team building and the importance of creative conflict. Good teams handle conflict well and with the hope that something better will emerge. As a team leader, ask yourself: What kinds of work teams will I create? Will there be trust? Similarly, what kinds of collegial relationships will I experience if people know ultimately they can't disagree with me? Good teams exist only where there can be healthy and respectful conflict.

Friends are also called to compassion, which means a no to fixing each other's pain.

This is a component of spending time together but isn't as self-evident as it might seem. It starts with the basic insight that we don't like pain. It's painful. So we try to avoid it. That means when we see friends in pain, we are tempted to fix them. Here's why psychologically: If we fix them, it seems that we've constructed a boundary around their suffering. We manage their pain. Then ultimately (we think) we're protected from pain. Here's an example: We hear that a friend's son is addicted to heroin. Our friend is despairing. So, instead of listening and opening up a space for their suffering, we begin to formulate a specific diagnosis: *It all started because her husband works too much. Besides that, she didn't spank her son as a baby. Then, when he was a teenager, she let him play in that garage band. And then . . .*

That's where we need to stop because we're beginning to seal our friends off from real love. You see, if we can diagnose the problem and figure out how she's responsible for her son's failings, then life is controllable. If we can offer an easy, self-evident fix, then we know *why* she is hurting. And then it won't happen to us, because we're smarter than that. The sad truth is that life cannot always be controlled; sometimes good marriages fail, caring parents have substance-abusing kids, and athletes die of heart attacks. The classic biblical book on pain, Job, states it with piercing brevity: "A mortal, born of woman, few of days and full of trouble, comes up life a flower and withers." That is, every woman and man will face distress and sorrow. Our goal as friends is not to fix and end the pain—that is generally futile—but to open up a space where our friend's pain can be brought and held. There healings can take place.

Friends are committed to a good greater than their personal pleasure, namely, to each other's best.

This no of friendship means a commitment to higher standards. The ancient Greek philosophical giant Aristotle laid it out well. He described a threefold component to friendship. It involves enjoying each other's company, receiving a benefit from the other's friendship, and being committed to the Good. The first two elements in Aristotle's view of friendship continue in our day, but do friends today understand the importance of this third component? We've all heard teenagers brought down by "peer pressure." We need to find friends who bring us up and therefore help us find what we are created to be.

At this point, many people will draw back: "I don't want someone meddling in my life." To some extent, I agree. I would certainly warn against seeking this kind of friendship if it's not based on mutual agreement. So don't speak to someone's faults unless you've been invited—doing so is a bad idea, and it rarely works. (In my profession, when someone who doesn't know me declares, "God told me something," my general rule is not to pay close attention.) In many ways, I don't like unsolicited advice either. I don't hunt for randomized criticism. I don't want someone to condemn me. But I've found that fear misses the point of Aristotle's call for friends to seek the Good: This is devotion to common goals. This is a "running partner" who keeps our pace in the course of life, someone on your team who is not staring you down but running alongside.

Here's how that functions in my life. Recently, I spent some time with a friend of over twenty years—a friend who has walked with me through difficult times, a friend who shares my often weird, and often arcane, profession of pastor. The time together was fabulous—renewing, affirming, reassuring, and strengthening. Above all, we not only enjoyed hanging out but also felt free to call each other to higher commitments—devotion to the craft of our profession and to pursuing integrity and excellence. In doing so, we mutually committed ourselves to saying no to mediocrity and compromise. Nonetheless, I find myself open to someone "getting in my business" only when I know I'm loved and valued by that person. And when I do, I realize this: This kind of friendship is unnerving, but whatever real success I've achieved is due in large measure to those who love me and keep me true to my commitments.

One final note: we need to say no to caring only for our friends and say yes to the call of service.

To follow Putnam's analysis one step further, I will point out that there are two kinds of social capital: *bonding*, which happens between the like-minded and which has been the bulk of this chapter; and *bridging*, which jumps over barriers and connects people separated by economics, ethnicity, age, and the like. My contention here is that sufficient bonding social capital sets us up for valuable bridging social capital—which, in my opinion, our culture desperately needs and which is necessary for our flourishing as human beings. In fact, as a Christian, I believe that God calls us to recognize the divine image in all those who bear it—and that's everyone. We are called to love our neighbor, which is reasonably self-evident. Jesus, in his poignant story about the Good Samaritan, taught that our neighbor is not just the person who is like us but anyone in need. He coached us not simply to *bond* with those who are like us but to make *bridges*. Altruism—giving across boundaries—as I've already noted, is good for us. It's the way we're made.

The icon of the civil rights movement, Martin Luther King, recognized the importance of caring for others. He once challenged his listeners with this:

> Everyone can be great because anyone can serve. You don't have to have a college degree to serve. You don't have to make your subject and verb agree to serve. You don't have to know about Plato and Aristotle to serve . . . you only need a heart full of grace. A soul generated by love. And you can be that servant.

Every great spiritual leader has told us that we need to reach out beyond ourselves in order to be fully human. And friends help us: Good friendships strengthen us so that we'll move beyond what's comfortable.

So let's say yes to friendship because friends are central to a successful life and they are precious, so we need to guard our friendships with many other nos. In the next chapter, I address how the power of no applies to families and allows our children and ourselves to find restraint so that we might thrive. But first I offer a few practical steps for nurturing our friendships.

A Friendship Assessment

A few questions will help you assess how much you want friends in your life. You might try sipping a cappuccino and thinking them through as acoustic guitar music plays in the background (funny, that's what I'm doing right now), or talking them through with your spouse or maybe even a friend. You might also grab a few sheets of paper or your laptop to make some journal entries.

1. First the "gut check" question: Do you really want to take time for friendships? Or does it take too much time away from work and your personal achievements? Friendships, like anything of value, require time and commitment.

2. Take a moment for gratitude, to count your blessings: What are those times when friends have encouraged you? Remember how it feels to be loved and affirmed. Send an e-mail, call, or write a bona fide letter to communicate your appreciation.

3. Look over a month on your calendar or PDA. How much time is there for friendships? Is there a sense of priority? Or are you too spread out, dabbling in friendship, but never really committing?

4. You can probably maintain no more than a half-dozen reasonably intimate friendships and about six more less intense ones. Who are those people? Try checking your cell phone and see the six people you dial most. Is that the list you'd like to focus on? Take that sheet of paper, or begin with an empty Word document, and write out the names of those friends whom you want to be central in your life.

CHAPTER NINE

Families Who No

*When I was a boy of fourteen, my father was so ignorant I
could hardly stand to have the old man around. But when
I got to be twenty-one, I was astonished at how much
he had learned.*

—MARK TWAIN

Everything I know about parenting I learned from the front
page of a July 2002 *Wall Street Journal*. Well, not exactly,
but there I did discover some insights from Ben Porter, an executive coach with clients like GM and Home Depot, especially
his concept of a "Family 360." (In case this is new language, 360
reviews involve managers and executives receiving feedback not
only from their superiors but also from those they supervise and
their peers—and even from themselves.) Porter's LeaderWorks
has developed the model of Family 360s for executives to see
how they're doing not just at work but at home. Porter explains

why: "These are the guys who have made their money many times over. More times than not, they've screwed up on the family side."

In fact, Porter ran a Family 360 for himself and received a number of surprises from his family. "You travel too much." "You're too distracted from us." And this choice reply: "Play more Frisbee." This didn't resemble any other 360 reviews he'd done for businesses. In fact, as the article noted, performance reviews can be intimidating, but it seems that the most demanding reviews come from our families.

This chapter offers a way to review our families through saying yes to no. With the power of no, we can extricate ourselves from the illusion that we need to be perfect parents with flawless children. It gives us freedom from selfishness and offers the flexibility of forgiveness. It helps us discover the freedom of a mature and excellent life.

Nonetheless, I offer this disclaimer: The gains come at some cost because often families and parenting present difficulties. It's often so painful that we don't want to look. Porter himself found that to enact these goals required no, especially no to self-seeking. Nurturing a family implies a no to self as the sole recipient of care and attention. For example, in his case, responding to the Family 360 required painful financial losses. He also grasped that he had to say no to himself: " 'Porter, you can't burn the candle at both ends. You're not fooling anybody . . .' There are big chunks of money I'm saying good-bye to. But I have a few more years before my kids are gone, and there's no going back." These nos will mean less income, but consequently Porter acquired something priceless. The Family 360 wasn't easy, but it was good. Porter grasped that the ability to create important values strengthens his—or anyone else's—work: "At the end of the day, the best-balanced people are the best executives." (The best executives are also the best-balanced people.)

In this chapter, I'm facing the daunting and complicated topic of families in three thousand words or fewer. So I'm approaching this topic with immense simplicity. In fact I'm declaring a no to saying everything there is to say. Instead, I'll just present a few applications of the power of no, including saying no to your children, which offers them necessary restraint and allows them to flourish.

This leads me to a simple analogy: Children are kites that need the string of restraint and the wind of their own initiative. Then they can fly. Without the restraint, they shimmy away in the wind. The power of no offers boundaries so that your kids can grow and mature. On the other hand, at certain times, we also need to say no to controlling our kids. It is a delicate balance, but without the wind of freedom, children stay grounded.

I'll unfold this principle in simple steps. And the first couldn't be simpler.

You are the parent; they are the children.

I write this unbelievably basic statement because many of us grew up in post–Dr. Spock parenting, when an odd application of the "child-centered" parenting might lead us parents to cower before the idea of asserting any parental authority. But, believe it or not, that's part of the job.

Yes, there are certainly nos that you must pronounce. No, you can't cut your little sister's hair with the weed whacker. No, one meal out of three has to move outside the food groups of sugar, artificial flavoring, and Cheez-Its. That kind of thing . . . We have to establish boundaries and rules that protect our children.

In fact, children need the boundaries that their parents set up. It's scary for kids when they make the rules. It's even scarier for the parents when they do!

Bless your kids. And remember the 5–1 ratio.

I realize "blessing" is an old word, but I think it's apt in this way: It used to be symbolized by laying our hands on our son's head and saying, "May God bless you." In this way, we were endorsing and sending our children out into the world. And I believe that every single child wants to know that her parents love and bless her. For that reason, I try (though often fail) to use the 5–1 ratio. For every one correction I make—"Chew with your mouth closed," "Make sure you scooped the cat poop," "Have you finished your homework?"—I seek to utter five times as many statements of gratitude (and I won't make it fifteen here, but these are a few examples): "Melanie, you are really creative," "Elizabeth, I appreciate your honesty," "Thanks for working hard at taking care of our animals," "I'm just thankful to be your father," "As far as I'm concerned, you're fabulous as you are."

Think of the ongoing importance of being blessed as children. I've come to realize that we all want a blessing from our parents, even as adults. Some of us never received it, and all we ever got was a pile of unrealistic expectations heaped on us. So we search throughout our lives for some surrogate blessing. I know I've seen fifty-something women still looking for their fathers to say, "Yes. You're good enough. You're pretty." Sometimes I think that's also the basis of men's gatherings from beer-drinking fraternities, to Robert Bly's drum-banging sessions, to the stadium-filled fervor of Promise Keepers. They want support from other men because their fathers never provided it. Some never got that word of encouragement. Some others received it, but like sweet milk from a baby's bottle, they have never been weaned. Either way, they're crying because they don't have right now what they want from their parents. And at some point it's time to let go of demanding their approval. Sometimes you have to tell them you don't need their advice anymore. It may even be time to forgive them.

And that's the issue I see with unnecessary frequency in families. Too many people are still crying about parents—rebelling against those who are long dead. We need to stop complaining and figure out what to do. Then we begin to live a free life. Not until we stop grumbling about our parents can we really enter into the potential of our own lives.

I'm reminded of a vignette from one of C. S. Lewis's Chronicles of Narnia in which Lewis's brilliant mind weaves psychological depth with poignant clarity. In the installment *The Silver Chair*, one of his favorite characters, Jill, has just experienced tragedy. She's burdened by despair and starts to cry. She remains paralyzed. The narrator then offers this insight: "Crying is all right in its way while it lasts. But you have to stop sooner or later and then you still have to decide what to do." Only when Jill figures out what to do can the story proceed.

This conviction comes primarily from my professional experience. As a pastor, I have met an unusual number of women and men who still live in rebellion against their parents' authority. Instead of saying no directly, these adult children rebel against voices and people no longer around. If indeed they are no longer around, it's time to let go of the anger. It's time to stop crying and figure out what to do—namely, to forgive and move on.

The key is that once we forgive our fathers and mothers, we can really begin to love them. And, conversely, until we forgive them, we'll never learn to love them. *Them*—our fathers and mothers, some of whom belittled us, physically abused us, or neglected us, others of whom got distracted from central tasks, and every single one of whom made mistakes.

This also relates to a more general conviction about parenting: It's about working oneself out of a job—not "raising kids" but "raising adults." I know what I want for my daughters. I want them to be honest, faithful, generous, and loving. I want them to feel blessed by me and Laura. As we take in the yes of what we seek our children to become when they're mature, we can say no to wanting immature children forever. Put simply, we are called to create children who don't depend on us for the rest of our lives.

This should be our blessing to them.

Parenting books provide only the structure in which you improvise.

Say no to following every jot and tittle from the books you read about parenting. (I'm returning to the topic of jazz leadership.) The central problem with those books is that they give us the distorted picture that somewhere there's a perfect family, perfectly applying the principles of parenting. They're not having the argument over whether you're being fair when you just wanted to have a nice family dinner together. They're not losing their cool when outdoor-only spray adhesive is used in a very indoor office space.

So say no to perfectionism in this case, the drive to be the perfect parent. If you're worried that your family's not like the one in the handbooks on family, you've already lost the battle. That family doesn't exist. (Or if it does, I don't want to know about it. That would lead to envy and lots of money spent on anger management.)

The power of no offers freedom by restraining our desire to control our kids. And as parents let's say no to obsessive control.

Our job as parents is to help our children find their voices. There is perhaps nothing sadder than children whose spirits have been stomped out by their parents. "He likes computers, but I'm a sports guy. So he'd better play Little League." Do you know what that feels like?

We need to say no to ourselves, especially to the sick, twisted desire to live through our kids. (Did I state that too strongly?) Our children will never be perfect. They are flawed human beings who can be rebellious, selfish, and deceitful. I remember tennis parents, when I played in the juniors, berating their kids after they were defeated in a three-hour match. Clearly the parents' egos were tied up in the win.

Let's do this differently: Let's free our children from our desire that they end up at Harvard or Stanford. (Actually, as a Berkeley grad, I prefer the first option.) They will not make more money than Bill Gates and give you 50 percent for your eighteen years of parenting. No, loving and nurturing your children will require forgiveness for actual misdeeds and, probably more, for their not living up to your expectations.

So say no to what you've always wanted them to be, and observe what skills and passions they actually have. Your children have gifts that are unique and yet are as fragile and beautiful as butterfly wings. Don't mangle your children, but let them be both flawed and gifted.

Learn to forgive your parents and your children for not being perfect.

What is forgiveness? That act of saying no to resentment is so critical to healthy families it requires a bit of elaboration. "Forgiveness," to quote the psychologist Frederic Luskin, "is about today." In other words, take the demands of today's hurts and seek to release them, not to hit back. Then, when we state a direct no to our parents' false expectations, we live for the grand yes of meaning, purpose, and maturity. Then we are able to forgive our children for the hurts they cause us.

After completing a dissertation in Stanford University's psychology department, in 1998 Luskin received a sizable grant that allowed him to assemble the largest forgiveness study ever. In the early stages of research, he asked Protestants and Catholics from Northern Ireland—mothers and immediate families of those killed in these conflicts—to begin to forgive. He defined forgiveness as releasing the anger and attaining emotional wellness. For Luskin, forgiveness does not mean reconciling, or forgetting (here I think he's not gone far enough), or saying what happened was okay (full agreement here). Using this group, he found a "significant" increase in optimism coupled with decreases in stress and depression. (In statistical studies of this kind, "significant" means to a greater degree than could have been simply chance.) He rechecked these changes through questionnaires after six months, and the results stayed the same.

Later, the American Express Company solicited Luskin to train a team of sales advisers in forgiveness. He categorized forgiveness under "emotional competence," that is, "navigating the world with flexibility and grace." (After a one-day training in forgiveness with these Am Ex sales advisers, Luskin began to track the results: The company found an 18 percent increase in sales performance and a 25 percent reduction in stress. By my lights, that's pretty instructive.)

Forgiveness in families is exceedingly more difficult than forgiveness in business, but the payoff is correspondingly greater. Remember first that your children are flawed. Hold them lightly and give them grace. In the end, forgiving them leads us to healthier lives. It also allows us to say a no to demanding perfection from our parents and offers a yes to healthy relationships and vigorous lives. So let's say no to demanding flawless excellence. Then we can find meaning, significance, and health for our families and for us. In addition, we must say no to our own extended infantile thinking and yes to true adulthood. When we learn to say healthy nos to our children and our parents and ourselves, we realize a new freedom to be who we are called to be.

In the next chapter, I bring the power of no to bear on marriage and the way it creates a hedge for romantic love to flourish. There we can discover the joy of a true soul mate. First, I offer some exercises to become families who no.

Review Your Family

1. Try a 360 review with your family. Ask them how you're doing and what areas need improvement. Remember to do a self-review.
2. Ask a friend to tell you where you indulge your children too much. What nos are needed for them to grow up as healthy adults?
3. Think back to some significant moment in your life when your parents really hurt you. Write down the feelings—see where you can find compassion and forgiveness. How are you doing with forgiving them at this point in your life? A simple chart will help this process. In three parallel columns, list significant moments when you were hurt by your parents, how you felt as a result, and how you now feel about forgiveness in each case.

4. Do you need to forgive your parents? Remember that "forgiveness is about today." Take time with a trusted friend or professional counselor. Learn to move on.

5. Reflect on a time when your parents affirmed you. Take time to let it go and don't demand that they continue to say, "Way to go." It's time to grow up and move on.

CHAPTER TEN

Marriage
To Know, You've Got to Say Yes to No

> *Like everything which is not the involuntary result of*
> *fleeting emotion but the creation of time and will, any*
> *marriage, happy or unhappy, is infinitely more interesting*
> *than any romance, however passionate.*

—W. H. AUDEN, twentieth-century poet and writer

———————————•———————————

The great ancient Greek philosopher Plato recounts a profound myth. In the famous dialogue called *The Symposium*,
or the "dinner party," he describes how each of us is only half
a soul. Plato says that we are incomplete, seeking fulfillment in
a soul mate, and we spend our lives searching for the other half.
When we find that other half, we come to completion. And
when this happens, we know it. More vernacularly—and moving down the intellectual food chain just a bit—this yearning
and discovery are summarized in the line from the film *Jerry*

Maguire when Tom Cruise's and Renée Zellweger's characters finally declare their love for each other with the succinct line "You complete me." You complete me—somehow you round out, and complement, who I am. That's a soul mate.

Similarly, the second chapter of Genesis—in words that would form our Western civilization's understanding of marriage—describes how the first man, Adam, watched God make all the animals. He even names every living thing. But he's still lonely. No creature is like him. No one stands beside him and shares life with him. The story then recounts the cry of Adam's joy when God creates Eve: "This at last is bone of my bones and flesh of my flesh."

A soul mate is the overpowering cry of our hearts. Meeting this need constitutes the deepest reason for marriage because soul mates draw out what's best and truest in each other. They can say to each other, "Thank you. I am more myself because of you."

The second chapter of Genesis continues by describing the completion of Adam's discovering his soul mate with the word "know." The phrase "Adam knew Eve" is a description not simply of the ecstasy and gift of sexual intercourse but also of a more comprehensive and personal knowledge. A soul mate really knows you, all components of what make you unique. Soul mates are the promise of a good marriage, and good marriages entail a sustained application of the power of no. In order to truly know another, you've got to say yes to no.

In the months following September 11, news agencies reported people rekindling their marriages. Divorce trials were postponed or abandoned. Couples intending to marry finally took the step. During that period of crisis, it seemed that Americans realized the shortness of time we all face and wanted to live in committed relationships. Nonetheless, in the years following, it seems that we're slipping back. We're becoming lazy about our relationships and complacent about our commitments. Will it take another colossal tragedy for us to wake up?

For a few reasons, this is not an easy chapter to write. It's not that I'm not for marriage. Because I am. It's not that I don't see happy marriages. Because I do. It's about other realities. First of all, few elements in our cultural environment support marriage. In fact, recent surveys suggest that a lower percentage of Americans are married than ever in the history of our country. Marriages in movies and books are considered generally "the ball and chain"—hindrances to self-expression and happiness. Instead, we're told that we find enduring bliss in the amazing surge of "falling in love" or "hooking up" in an unexpected sexual encounter. I don't contest the beauty of the feelings, or the power of the surge of biochemicals, but they won't endure.

Of course, there is a fascination with marriage in "reality TV"—with *The Bachelor, The Ultimate Love Test,* and such. They demonstrate that a particular question continues to fascinate our culture: Can marriages, in our contemporary society, work? Our entertainers deny it. Listen to two actors. (Here's another mystery: Movie stars are the sages of our time. Why? They're taught to recite what others write. Therefore they have astute insights into the issues of our times. I guess that makes sense. But I digress . . .) Rosanne Barr once declared that marriage is bad for women, and the day before I first typed this chapter, I overheard Jim Carrey on a nearby TV opine that marriage may not function anymore because "everyone's out for the brass ring." Ergo marriage obstructs our path to personal advancement. And that's what it's all about.

But I still believe that a committed relationship is where we flourish. I also am convinced that the power of no can make a critical difference in helping marriages succeed and I believe offers a hedge in which romantic love can blossom.

To address the topic of marriage, I've organized this chapter into three nos, each of which leads to a greater promise:

- No to infidelity.
- No to marriage as mere therapy.
- No to selfish achievements.

With these nos in place, the promise is that married life together can be an amazing yes that blends commitment and passion.

The first no is to infidelity.

Simply put, we are not living out fidelity to marriage. In other words, Americans are, by and large, finding it terribly difficult not to slip out of the commitment to sexual faithfulness.

Previously, Western societies thought that adultery was important in breaking up marriages. In fact, adultery a few decades ago possessed a stigma similar to child abuse today because of its effect on society. Perhaps that's too strong. Still, a few years ago, I was surprised to learn that New Jersey, like many other states, does not include sexual infidelity as grounds for divorce. I'm not debating the law here, but our legal codes do signify cultural shifts. It seems that we've forgotten that unfaithfulness breeds distrust. We tend to think, like Emma Bovary and her literary lovers in Gustave Flaubert's novel, that extramarital sexual liaisons arise from boring and miserable unions. Interestingly enough, *sexual infidelity doesn't necessarily follow marital discontent; it often creates it.* Consider the 56 percent of men who have engaged in affairs and yet reported that their marriages were happy. Nevertheless, after their affairs, the marriages suffered. I've also been told by a therapist that women who commit adultery almost never go back to a healthy marriage. They've checked out emotionally.

But affairs are so easy—not only the full-blown sexual ones, but even the subtle emotional affairs. It starts with holding hands while having drinks at a conference, or taking a little more time at lunch with a colleague, or hugging someone just a little more than is warranted. These choices gradually, softly, and without fanfare lead us away from our commitments.

Admittedly, it's common to desire people other than one's spouse. Our sexually saturated advertising culture really doesn't help (nor of course does logging on to Internet porn, but that's pretty obvious). Besides that, sometimes we just become bored. And we're pumped full of the motto that boredom is the worst form of evil, followed by the sin of "repressing" a craving. But not every desire has to be served, a thought that runs counter to the prevalent American slogan—which I know is important because I read it on a T-shirt—"It's all about me." For a marriage to work, we can't simply revolve around *my* desires and *my* wants.

What I'm saying is that marriage calls us to say no to a level of adolescent indulgence. And the United States currently seeks to live in perpetual adolescence. Once again, our movies are revealing—they largely describe adolescent "coming of age." But adolescence is pure, unrestrained individualism. And though individualism is valuable, it has to find a counterpoint in commitment. In their book, *Habits of the Heart: Individualism and Commitment in American Life,* a team of five sociologists led by the respected Berkeley professor Robert Bellah analyzed our country's drive for self-fulfillment and self-expression and its effect on the social institutions that connect us. In one section, this team focused on marriage, and they discovered—partly to their surprise—that few Americans outside of evangelical Christians could describe why they were married outside of "It's good for me." Marriage goes beyond being good "for me"; it should also be good for my spouse, good for my children, and even good for society. Evangelicals apparently decided that marriage was important for others besides themselves and that it ultimately represented a commitment to God, and that these responsibilities surpassed their feelings. "Only by having an obligation to something higher than one's own preference or one's own fulfillment, [these evangelicals] insist, can one achieve a permanent love relationship." They found that the will to stay together is more important than blissful feelings about our marriages. Sometimes a no to what feels good achieves a yes to something more important. And, I believe, this is one truth our country desperately needs to hear.

Let's be clear: I'm not asking to repeal divorce laws. Certainly some marriages are abusive or more generally so destructive that they have to end. But here I'm arguing for those who want to keep their marriage healthy. So I ask the question, What happens when it's no longer "good for me" and someone who caters better to your sexual needs arrives? Our culture needs something like sexual self-restraint throughout life to keep marriages healthy.

Let's try a thought experiment. What about those who start with abstinence as a preparation for marriage and the sexual self-restraint a successful marriage requires? Sadly, that alternative is hardly included in our "inclusive" culture. I was surprised to discover a 2005 *New York Times* article describing "yet another alternative lifestyle" at Princeton University promoted by the Anscombe Society. Their mission? To promote the traditional sexual values of chastity and abstinence outside of marriage. The university seemed bemused and ill prepared for these students' views. One nineteen-year-old, Jennifer Mickel, a sophomore

from Monroe, Louisiana, relates her experience. She found herself at a meeting of the Ivy Council, an Ivy League intercampus
group:

> The discussion was very sex-focused, like about having
> rape kits in medical centers and condoms and the morning-
> after pill. And I asked, "What do your schools have for
> women who are not having sex?" And the room fell si-
> lent. These delegates are appointed by their schools to be
> experts on these subjects, and no one had anything to say
> about abstinence.

Could university campuses allow for saying no in this form?
And might it even be necessary?

Naturally, this level of self-restraint runs counter to pop culture. Could it be that the ultimate offense to our consumer society is to say no to some type of pleasure? We have to realize
that marriage is something to be not consumed but savored, and
if marriage is to be sustained, there must be some nos stated,
especially the no to self.

Marriages are no mere therapeutic relationships.

I just read through my personal journal from 2001, which
described the events leading to that visit to the cardiologist I discussed in the introduction. As Laura and I were spinning more
and more into discontent, we sought the insights of counseling. A good idea, to be sure—one I've recommended to many
couples. Therapy, as I'm defining it, is characterized by a "non-
judgmental" relationship between therapist and client, where
it's important "to be heard," but where advice and—perish the
thought!—identification of guilt are spurned.

But here's an example from 2001: Our counselor's best advice for our marriage was "It's so good that you're able to express your emotions so well. That's where the health of the marriage will be found. So let's hear more." My response. *What? That's it! Thanks for that piece of pop psychology. What other beautiful, $120-an-hour thoughts do you have for us today?*

But certainly for us and for many couples, there's a more fundamental issue: What happens when both spouses "express their emotions," and they're both needy? Who wins? I return to Howard Crossland, a scientist and evangelical Christian whom the Habits of the Heart team interviewed. He offered this: "I have a sign hanging in my bedroom: 'Love is when another's needs are greater than your own.' "

Maybe Howard Crossland can save us $120 an hour. Sometimes expression of emotions does not suffice. You have to put aside your needs and then solve the problem. Say no to something you're demanding. Make a concession. Look to the intentions and commitments *behind* the presenting problem. Then seek a higher resolution than your own desires. Solve the problem, not just the feelings about the problem.

Say no to a life of selfish achievements and yes to the good of interdependence.

I think Plato was onto something in describing our search for a soul mate. We all deeply desire that person who will help us move from self-seeking to caring and serving. In a good marriage, we learn to move from independence to interdependence.

I remember a bus ride up Columbus Avenue in New York City with my friend Max, an intelligent twenty-something young man. He and I were discussing marriage and particularly his current relationship. With a father who asked at the end of every phone call, "Are you the first one to arrive at work and the last one to leave?" Max was very career driven. As he described the ups and downs he was experiencing with his girlfriend, he made a statement I'll probably never forget: "We don't have enough time for a relationship."

That was entirely honest, but more than a little tragic. Taking time for a relationship takes *time*, and when we do, our soul mates actually help us find who we really are. It's the value of friendship notched up at least a degree or two. And we will never find a soul mate until we move beyond that kind of self-seeking. Thankfully, Max knew it, too. I was able to officiate at his wedding just two weeks after September 11.

These nos lead to the profound yes of marriage: the need to bring together the two halves of love, passion and commitment.

As a minister, I celebrate at a variety of weddings. Every time—because I have the best seat in the house—I ponder the faces of the bride and the groom. Dressed in a beautiful gown and a crisp tuxedo, often with tears rolling down their nervously expectant faces, they look longingly into each other's eyes. Even with worries about the amount of responses for the reception, dysfunctional family dynamics, gifts for the bridesmaids and groomsmen, and reservations for the honeymoon, there's still a moment where most get it. They focus. They realize that the wedding day is unique. At the critical point in the ceremony—their vows—they pledge themselves to each other. And even if every wedding service doesn't cite the Book of Common Prayer, the phrase "forsaking all else" is implied. The husband and wife agree to let go of other romantic relationships, other future lovers, for the sake of sanctifying their bond and cultivating their life with each other.

Certainly too many don't live up to their promises, and the results are tragic. Lives are broken, children fought over, and husbands and wives separate (whether legally or simply emotionally). But when they learn how to say no, when they live out "forsaking all else" and thus say yes to each other, that indeed is a different story. A successful marriage begins.

On that day, here's what I offer as the best way to describe the goodness of nurturing a soul mate through marriage.

God has created the passion that brings together a woman and a man. Indeed it's a God-given human experience that our culture celebrates. This is intense desire for each other that's well summarized in the biblical poem the Song of Solomon, which uses the imagery of fire as a metaphor for passionate love:

Love is as strong as death
passion as fierce as the grave.
Its flashes are flashes of fire, a raging flame.
Many waters cannot quench love, neither can floods
    drown it.

So married couples need to remember to fan the flames of passion. Sometimes we are so happy to "win" each other that we can forget the ongoing need to court each other for all the years to come. It's actually critical to remember to take time for dinners together, for long conversations, and for luxurious walks along the Champs-Élysées in Paris . . . or maybe Main Street in Chico, California.

But passion cannot stand without the second component of love, namely, commitment. The classic description of committed love is found in the New Testament, from the pen of Saint Paul:

> Love is patient; love is kind; love is not envious or boast-
> ful or arrogant or rude. It does not insist on its own way;
> it is not irritable or resentful; it does not rejoice in wrong-
> doing, but rejoices in the truth. It bears all things, believes
> all things, hopes all things, endures all things.

Without the fuel of that type of love, the flame of passion would flare up and fizzle. These two sides of love need to be wedded to create an enduring marriage.

What other resources does a couple have? First of all, their commitment to a lasting love cannot stand without the support of family and friends around them. These people are gifts that couples give each other. They are divine gifts, means by which God supports your marriage. Family and friends stand as witnesses, as cheerleaders, and as counselors. And beneath all this—like gigantic hands supporting marriages—God holds up the vows of marriage because God designed and supports marriage. According to the Jewish Scriptures, God is indeed a God who makes and keeps promises. This is in fact celebrated in the Hebrew word for "steadfast love," *chesed*, as in the biblical book of Isaiah:

> For the mountains may depart and hills be removed,
> But my *chesed* shall not depart from you,
> And my covenant of peace shall not be removed,
> Says the Lord, who has compassion on you.

I close with an image. I've mentioned earlier the distinctive quality of jazz, improvisation, the spontaneous expression of creativity. Yet, as a jazz musician, I can tell you that all the spontaneity in the world doesn't come from simply sitting down at the drums and banging away. We've all heard that, and whatever it is, it's not music. Instead, great improvisation is built on a pledge to practice drum rudiments, day in and day out, year after year. The amazing discovery is not just that drummers can play musically but that out of all this discipline they (like other musicians) develop spontaneity. They begin playing "from the heart." Improv happens when the spontaneity of the moment and the commitment of hours of practice come together.

You can probably see where this is leading. I've already described our work as improvisation. Here, in marriage, passionate love is bounded by the nos implicit in the vows to seek each other's best. In marriage, passion and commitment ultimately play off each other. Those two create a love that lasts. These two halves of love—and the two soul mates coming together—create a rich, beautiful harmony.

Some Practical Steps: Blessing Your Marriage

I had the opportunity to celebrate two weddings on the *Today* show. Because it was television, I needed to craft every phrase very carefully because when you're given three minutes and forty-five seconds to describe the meaning of a life lived together, you want to make every word count! So I worked hard with this blessing, which closed one of these ceremonies. I've built off the insights of others and sought to define succinctly what it means to find—and celebrate—your soul mate.

Meditate on these words and see how this describes your relationship, how you might want it to be, or perhaps even one you would like:

May God bless you and keep you.

May the love that you so clearly have for one another hold you close

And may it flourish for years to come.

May your dreams come true.

But when they don't, may you cry with one another and stand by one another

Until new dreams arise in their place.

So that, many years from now you may be able to look at one another

And you'll be able to say this:

"Because of you I lived the life I always wanted to live.

"Because of you I became the person that I always wanted to be."

Amen.

Then take some time—perhaps over a weekend by the beach or at the mountains together—to discuss some topics:

- What is working well in your marriage? Count the blessings.
- It's always better to start from strength. So how will you continue to cultivate these strengths?
- What needs improvement? And here the focus is not complaining but clearly describing your needs. "I need a little more time with you, simply listening." "I need to be valued by you. So be careful about—and maybe even avoid—saying things to others that make me feel small and undervalued."
- Where is there conflict in your marriage? What problems are you and your spouse presenting to each other?

What lies *behind* these concerns? Can you resolve what
lurks behind the conflict that never seems to go away
by affirming the deeper values and dreams that you
and your spouse are seeking to protect?

- Write down three concrete steps you'll take to develop
your marriage.

Beyond Our Nos

The future ain't what it used to be.

—YOGI BERRA

————————————◆————————————

One final chapter needs to be written, and one last thing needs to be said: Life is more than no because no is not the ultimate utterance. That final word is yes.

Declare no to misery and yes to joy, to life, to health, to excellence, and to beauty. No, I will not let the pressures of life have the final word. No, I will not let controlling others dominate my relationships. No, I will not follow a false self. I will say yes to the way I have been created, to the path of true success, to hearing that deep inner voice. Yes, I will pursue my work with excellence, with a healthy rhythm, with integrity, and with improvisational freedom. Yes, I will choose good friendships and family relationships, and I will choose a healthy, enduring marriage. In the end—if we are to live mature and excellent lives—we must shift our focus from negation to affirmation. We say yes to no so that we can move from no to yes.

To write this book, I do have the settled conviction that no is an important word, one that our time needs to learn. I'm fairly sure that's clear. But I have to admit that no also first emerges with the "terrible twos," when toddlers realize they can set boundaries on their world. It continues into the notorious rebellion that defines adolescence. At some point, children yearn to determine their own paths and cast down some of the idols they've been given. By "idols" I'm pointing to ideologies and truths that our culture and parents hand us, behind which lurk philosophical and even theological commitments. Yet this can be dangerous. Our culture bows before the idols of irresponsibility and immaturity and many young people can become lost and disoriented. Our children need to be reminded that saying yes to no, though sometimes difficult, can lead to greater freedom and joy in their lives.

Ultimately our nos lead to a yes to how we are wired. And, by my lights, accepting how we are created implies a yes to God's intention. God can guide us to healthy personal lives, dynamic work, and vibrant relationships. God's intentions, God's yes, ought to shape our nos.

Now, with those last sentences, I'm sensing you might feel a slight amount of incredulity because they come from the mouth of a pastor, a "hired gun" for religion, as it were. Of course, I'm going to say that kind of thing. But what if I told you this: I don't say this is true because I'm a minister; I'm a minister because I believe it to be true?

Let me explain how I got to this conclusion.

I found God in Berkeley, California. Nursed on the casual secularism of the region now known as Silicon Valley, I grew up not needing God, but being satisfied by great weather, comfortable surroundings, and personal achievements. I was a happy secular Californian. I distinguish this from a Jean-Paul Sartre– nurtured atheistic existentialist, drinking French roast, wearing peg-leg jeans, and filling wire-bound journals with reflections on meaninglessness and the Abyss while dissonant Schoenberg symphonies fill the air. And so, not denying God, but also not considering God's existence relevant or useful, I found it easy to stroll the path set by a self-sufficient San Mateo County—a region, I'm told, where less than 10 percent of the residents are found in church on any given Sunday.

I remember my childhood as reasonably easy, with two hap- pily married parents and a supportive older brother. My family's court philosopher was Ayn Rand, the Russian-born immigrant who became zealously pro-American and who is probably best known for her novels *Atlas Shrugged* and *The Fountainhead*. In these books, and assorted nonfiction pieces, she constructed a philosophy of objectivism (the world out there really exists; it's no illusion), unabashed laissez-faire economics (which she builds on some rather unique ways of reading American economic his- tory), and ethics of selfishness and personal fulfillment (we live for ourselves, our pleasure, and our achievements). The phi- losophy proved stultifying in general—it's extremely rigid and inhumanly demanding—but this final element of what Rand termed the "virtue of selfishness" became its particular Achilles' heel for me.

If I had a theological creed, it was agnosticism or atheism. But it wasn't that explicit, relevant, or necessary. Instead, any signifi- cant metaphysical commitment lurked casually in the back of my mind. Nonetheless, I now realize the presence of this casual nonbelief held the seeds of a problem. Atheism is effectively one large no: "No, God does not exist. Or at least if God exists, it's impossible to prove or irrelevant to modern, intelligent adults.

Therefore, no, the universe lacks purpose or meaning." Or as the best-selling author Richard Dawkins phrases it, the universe is "nothing but blind, pitiless indifference." Thus atheism cannot solve one of its own dilemmas, namely, the problem of good: If there is at bottom no God and no purpose, why is there good in the world? Why is there meaning? Why can we perceive beauty? And why do we care?

Still, I found functional atheism acceptable enough until I arrived at UC Berkeley at age seventeen. There, for a variety of unforeseen reasons, I started looking into religion. "Grow up in a secular home. Go to Berkeley. Become a Christian." It doesn't make a lot of sense. But in Barth's words, it was time to overthrow one big idol, namely, Me at the center of the universe.

As a first-year student in this overwhelming university and pluralistic city, I was confused and undone by my newfound collegiate freedom. No parent or teacher could provide me with certainties, and quite frankly the old ones didn't work so well. The voice of self-sufficiency, objectivism, and selfish, personal fulfillment rang hollow. I found myself regularly strolling through Berkeley's famous Sproul Plaza—where Mario Savio jumped on a police car, initiating the Free Speech Movement in 1964—and on every side I was surrounded by the free and cacophonous voices of various student group tables. It was a veritable circus. All offered directions: the Spartacus Youth League, gay and lesbian empowerment, animal rights, medical cannabis use, Green Party sign-up, Berkeley Free Clinic, and the like.

What did intrigue me—through a few books and friends I'd encountered—was to check out God. Admittedly, this search wasn't purely intellectual—I've since learned that we don't engage arguments in abstraction, we engage with people we respect. And respectable Christians I found. We had arguments, discussions, and more arguments, by pools, at Denny's, and beside lockers. They handed me various books, many now forgotten, with the obvious exception of the Bible and C. S. Lewis, who—as you can see from this book—has left an indelible impression. His *Mere Christianity*, which describes his grounds for belief in God, got under my skin with its reasoned and reasonable approach to Christian faith.

I also took Religious Studies 90A, an introduction to the basic menu of religious traditions: the "world religions" of Hinduism, Buddhism, Judaism, Christianity, and Islam with a bit of animism and Chinese religion thrown in. As I began to read, I discovered that there was a pervasive reverence for Jesus among world faiths. Buddhism describes him as an "enlightened" figure. Hinduism easily fits him into its rather comprehensive worship of numerous deities. Islam considers him one of the prophets. Judaism? Well, that provided a fascinating exception and simultaneously the seedbed for his teachings. Of course, Christianity centers wholeheartedly on Jesus.

So many religions talked about Jesus, so why not read the primary texts about his life, the Gospels? (Remember, I had never really done that before.) As a student of literature I soon realized that Jesus, this central figure of the Gospels of Matthew, Mark, Luke, and John, wasn't some fictional protagonist. For one thing, his depiction honestly wasn't artful enough. Mark, for example, writes in very rough language. The Gospels included details that didn't necessarily carry the story along, but had the hard authenticity of history. And, on the other hand, Jesus's personality and actions kept "pushing back" against my preconceptions. He spoke and acted through the pages of the Bible. He wasn't just some nice Sunday-school kid, and he talked about things that I didn't like—serving others, shunning status, dying to self—and that didn't just appeal to my baser desires. He was no salesman.

Once he got under my skin, he didn't make things easier. In

fact, he intensified my discontent with a life of secular contentment and Randian selfishness. I realized that my ready-made
answers were insubstantial. Eventually, the character of Jesus
captured me. Without every answer clearly figured out, in Feb-
ruary 1981 I nonetheless admitted that in Jesus I found the big
yes to God, and I committed my life to following him. And that
great yes now defines all my nos.

And so today I'm looking at a very different future from when
this book began. Then I was in New York City, bracing myself against heart troubles and high blood pressure. During the
writing of *Say Yes to No* I moved to Chico, a bustling university
town of a hundred thousand in the upper Sacramento Valley,
poised between the foothills of the Sierra Nevada and the groves
of almonds. It's not terribly far from John Sutter's famous mill
that started the forty-niners seeking a glittery golden fortune.

As I finalized these reflections in Chico, I kept remembering
that there is more to life than surviving. Moving has been good.
It's a much better place for me in this chapter of life, holding
together the responsibilities of family, work, and my own goals
and dreams. I've discovered that no amount of positive thinking
will compensate for concrete changes that need to be made. I
know that sometimes using the power of no means you'll have
to make more than internal, psychological adjustments. Or
more precisely: When you've adjusted your attitude and things
still haven't righted themselves, it's time to look outside yourself.
Nonetheless—and if it needs to be stated—New York City is a
fabulous world-class city, and it certainly does not constitute an
impossible place to live. But for me and at this point in my life,
I had to say no in order to flourish.

I've attempted to internalize all the lessons of the power of
no. In my personal life, I've sought to chip away at the penultimate goods of wealth, fame, and position and to walk on the

right road. To do this, I'm practicing to use technology and not be used by it, so I can, as much as possible, center on the center. Weekly and daily, I (and Laura) have declared a no to work during certain times of the day, and we've sought the healthy rhythm of life established by Sabbath. I've been improvising, seeking out that glorious blend of form and flexibility to work creatively, while staying true to my principles, even when it's tough. Finally, I've also remembered the critical importance of relationships, saying no to a life without them. In my family, Laura and I have tried to combine freedom and restraint. In our marriage, we've worked hard to harness the power of no to create a place where our passion for each other can burn for years to come.

My only fear is that saying all this may sound a little too perfect. So it's important to admit that I'll probably always have a tendency toward hypertension, my job can still overwhelm me at times, and my children can be overly demanding. But when I say yes to no, I find an excellent and beautiful life. When I don't, it tends to slip from my grasp.

I left this chapter until the end because I'm convinced that the power of no works. Ultimately it's about finding a yes that resonates with who you are. In the end, I believe that's discovering how God created you. When you find your deepest joy, maybe then it will lead you to an even deeper yes.

In the final year of writing this book, I was on vacation with my family in Manhattan and made a trip one beautiful early June morning to Lexington and Seventy-fourth. On that urban sidewalk, I stood before a large plain beige building. I stepped up to a simple black door with a brass knob. A straightforward plate to the right read (with noteworthy alliteration), "Cornell

Cardiology Consultants." Indeed. I had returned to the office of Molly S. Stephenson, M.D., and her associates. Memories of that spring morning just a few years earlier gradually returned. Meaning no slight to Dr. Stephenson's work, I still confess that negative emotions emerged first: the sense of desperation and fear mingled with a mild hope that I could make a change, all bound together with confusion.

I stood there for a few more moments and pondered. Slowly I realized I didn't stand before those steps as the same person I was in March 2001. Whether or not I will visit a cardiologist again, I had changed. Potential dangers remained, but by saying yes to no I had set boundaries on many things that threatened health, integrity, and sanity and I had discovered the few things that bring meaning, significance, and purpose. I became even quieter and listened. I heard a voice declare yes.

When I start hearing voices at Seventy-fourth and Lex, I know it's time to take a break. And so, after that profound moment, I walked on and continued my vacation.

So, yes, as I wrote at the beginning of this book, I'm all right now. Saying yes to no has certainly helped . . . especially as it leads, beyond my no, to a more powerful, life-affirming yes.

ACKNOWLEDGMENTS

To acknowledge the role of some in this book's creation is to risk omitting others. Nonetheless, I'll forge ahead with the rubric "lean instead of luxurious" (to employ Earl Palmer's pithy phrase in a different context). First of all, a shout-out to my wife, Laura, and my two girls, Lizzie and Mel, for the rousing discussions over the past eight years about the proper role of no and yes in our lives (as well as opinions on the title, the colors of the cover, and a host of other themes). Similarly, I'm grateful for my parents, Ruth and Tom, for demonstrating the need for no and making room for yes, as well as for the friends who support me in seeking a sustainable and "sambalike" rhythm in life. They all put up with hearing about "the power of no" and "say yes to no" ad nauseam. (I suppose that's what friends and family are for.) In addition, I've enjoyed the support of some very worthy colleagues in the process of writing: Ken Giniger for early interactions on these topics; Bill Barry for his good humor, insight, and patience during months of careful chiseling on the manuscript;

John Burke, Trace Murphy, Andrew Corbin, and Gary Jansen for their various ways of supporting this project; and Barbara Hendricks and Dennis Welch for helping me craft this message and present it to a wider public. Finally—though I'm not sure if this fits the category of "acknowledgment"—I thank God for this *kairos* and for demonstrating that the final word is always yes, but that word requires a few nos along the way.

ABOUT THE AUTHOR

Greg Cootsona is a pastor at Bidwell Presbyterian Church in Chico, California. Formerly he ministered at the Fifth Avenue Presbyterian Church in New York City, where he headed the Center for Christian Studies. He has appeared on the *Today* show two times to officiate their annual wedding program. Greg is married and has two young daughters.